THE FOOTPRINTS OF GOD

Meditations on the Word of God

by

Francis Martin

Priest of Madonna House

DIMENSION BOOKS

Denville, New Jersey

First Edition
Published by Dimension Books, Inc.
Denville, New Jersey 07834

For My Mother. . .from whom

I received both the bread and the Word.

CONTENTS

Introduction 5
Matthew 1: 1-25 Mary, Quiet Flame 7
         2: 1-12 Follow Your Star 8
         2: 13-23 Patron Saint of the Real 11
         3: 13-17 He Who Hides 13
         6: 14-21 Footprints of God 15
         6: 22-32 He Trusted Too Much! 17
         8: 18-27 No Guts, No Glory! 19
         8: 28-34 Lord, You Make Us Nervous 22
         9: 1-8 Yes, Lord, I Think You Can 25
         9: 27-35 Always Room For. . . ? 27
        14: 22-34 Leaning On God 31
        18: 21-35 Love Doesn't Keep Score 33
        19: 16-26 Healing With Nothing 36
        20: 1-16 Rejoicing In God's Mercy 38
        22: 2-14 Mary Was God's Idea 41
        22: 1-14 Sorry, Not Interested 43
        24: 1-34 Parousia: Beginning of the End ... 45
        25: 31-40 Just Don't Be Surprised 48
        28: 16-20 The Family Life of God 49
Mark 1: 14-20 Hearing the New Song 51
      2: 1-12 On Carrying Each Other 54
      5: 1-15 The Presence of Christ 56
      7: 31-37 Healing Costs Something 58
      8: 34-9:1 God Is Deeper Than Pain 60
     10: 46-52 Truth Force 63
     15: 43-16:8 Anointing the Bodies of Christ 65
Luke 2: 41-52 Mary Looks For God 67
      4: 16-30 Just An Ordinary Guy 70
      5: 1-11 But We've Already Tried! 73
      8: 3-15 Letting the Seed Grow 75
      8: 40-48 Please Touch 77
     10: 23-37 Shifting the Center of Gravity ... 79

	10:	38-42 God and Man Are Not Rivals ...	83
	11:	14-27 Nothing Real Without Joy	85
	14:	15-24 Children of Mercy	87
	16:	1-13 No Time To Lose	89
	18:	9-14 God Is a Pushover	92
	19:	1-10 Zacchaeus Was For Real	95
	21:	20-28 First Flush of Dawn	98
John	1:	43-51 Icon of the Father	100
	2:	1-11 Longing Is Presence	102
	2:	13-17 Weep, Love, and Stay	105
	3:	13-17 Little Souls Just Get Wet	107
	4:	5-42 God's Will Is Our Measure	109
	6:	56-59 Dreams Come True	112
	8:	31-47 Christ the Abiding One	114
	9:	1-12 Losing Is Finding	116
	10:	22-30 The Gift of Christ's Love	119
	14:	18-31 The Poetry of God	121
	16:	16-28 What's In a Name?	123
	18:	33-38 The Kingdom of Truth	126
	20:	24-30 The Thomas In Us	128

INTRODUCTION

Origen said that preaching is breaking the bread of the Word for God's people. This book is meant to be an aid to, not a substitute for, the reading and the meditation of scripture. There is a passage noted before each meditation which should be read and prayed over. The meditation which follows is only meant to foster the action of the Spirit in each one's heart.

There is no particular plan to the readings. It neither follows the liturgical year nor is it a systematic treatment of the Gospels. There are fifty-two sections in case one would wish to use the book for weekly meditations throughout a year. Otherwise, it may simply be used when one has time. It is hoped that the reader will find refreshment for the spirit by reading and praying over the scriptures, and that some food for life may be found in the meditations.

Francis Martin
Madonna House
Combermere, Ontario

The writers of the Gospels, in good semitic fashion, were very intent on having us know who Jesus was, something about his family and tradition. In this Gospel we have a long list of names. Every once in a while we might recognize one of them. . .Isaac, Achaz, Isaiah, Solomon, maybe Jesse, the father of David. Salvation history is presented before our eyes. The list goes all the way through the bible. It starts with Abraham and goes to Jacob, the father of Joseph, the husband of Mary, of whom was born Jesus, who is called the Christ. All those centuries of preparation were gripped by the vision of something great coming.

What is the recounting of such a geneology trying to tell us? Certainly one thing: that God is not to be found very far away. Our Lord's ancestry, you know, was not the best. If you read the history of some of those kings whose names are mentioned, you will find that many of their lives were not very edifying, to say the least! Our Lord's own foster-father and mother were a scandal because they were so ordinary. We know that when Jesus went back to his own home town and preached one day, nobody would accept him. "We know who he is. Isn't his mother in the same town with us? Isn't his father the carpenter?"

When we reflect on the earthly origins of the Son of God, we begin to realize that all the generations who longed for his coming in a way "forced" him to come. Their hearts were on fire. The holy Mother of God herself so yearned for the presence of God among his people that God couldn't resist any longer. Generations of longing forced God's hand by the depth of their desire.

We know now what the longing was all about. We know in clear vision what all those great people who went before us only knew in a dim light. We know too that if we let our hearts desire salvation with the same intensity they did, we too will make God present among us. He cannot resist coming to hearts which long for him.

Mary, especially, was like a flame, the flame of a candle. A candle flame doesn't seem to be moving. But just get up close to it and put your hand out. You will soon enough experience the power and energy radiating from it. Maybe a flame is a good image of what we are supposed to be like. Like the Holy Family, we experience the scandal of ordinariness, the ordinariness of a candle flame. At the same time, it is a fire that could consume us if we would let it have its way with us. Mary is the perfect example of the "ordinary flame" that burned so intensely that God couldn't wait any longer. Such intensity will make him be born in our hearts as well.

Matthew 2: 1-12   *FOLLOW YOUR STAR*

Let us set aside for the moment any critical consider-ations of the exact nature of this text, that is, who the Magi may have been, how they ever got into the Gospel, the questions of "Midrash," and so on. We can then settle down into the central intention of St. Matthew and which has always been the center of the Christian tradition concerning these three men. They were three persons, three pilgrims, three kinds of people. What they represent is the coming to Christ of people who never shared even the Old Testament tradition out of which the Christ was born. They were three astrologers who came from the east, somewhere in Mesopotamia, and all they had to go by was something that they saw or thought they saw in the heavens.

They were faithful to what they saw. They followed their star and were even humble enough to ask people for directions once in a while. "Where is this Messiah, where is this king of the Jews to be born?" The people who answered their questions (who had all the answers!) had none of the deep love of truth that these three had. Nevertheless, the former contributed to the wisemen's discovery whether they knew it or not.

Three pilgrims, three kinds of people who had very little to go on, but who were faithful to that. Gentiles, non-knowers, pagans, the ones who weren't on the "in." Maybe today we would call them communists, the outsiders, those who are not "in the know" as far as faith is concerned—these are the people who were brought to Christ by something in the heavens.

As the Church looks upon them, these three men stand as the very symbol of faith. These three people who didn't have faith, in the sense of being brought up in the tradition, learned the meaning of faith because they were faithful to what they saw, and they followed it. These three astrologers, again, uninformed by any tradition, have become, throughout the whole Church, the symbol of contemplation. Contemplation is being held in the grip of great mysteries. These men were polarized by the truth that they followed, and they followed "with great joy."

The word joy occurs three times in the text. They rejoiced because they saw a star. They didn't even know where it was going to lead, or what was going to be at the end of their journey. The star led them to Christ. And the minute they contacted Christ they fell down and worshipped, and they opened up all their treasures and gave them to him, gave them, not to a great potentate, but to a Child.

The application is painfully obvious. How often we say to ourselves, "If only I had more faith. If I had more faith I could do a lot." We already have all we need. What we are supposed to do is *act* on what we see, and on *all* that we see. There are times in our lives when Christ does

not appear too clearly as the star. All we see is a dim
reflection of Christ hovering over us. But it is true, and we
know it's true, but we stand there saying, "If only I had
more faith, more light. If only Christ himself would
appear, I could continue with the next step of my
journey." And so we just stand there, waiting.

Yet, these three gentlemen, who probably never
heard of Moses or Jeremias, were just analyzing stars. They
only saw a glimpse of the truth, but they followed it.
Matthew's Gospel says that they were the first to reach
Christ; in another Gospel it is the shepherds. It is the Magi
who have become for us a symbol of faith and a symbol of
prayer. Like them, we must be able to follow a star and
rejoice when we catch sight of it, no matter if it's among
clouds or not. All we are supposed to do is *follow it*.

When you think about it, everybody else seemed to
have more knowledge, more light than they did. Everybody else seemed to know where Christ was going to be
born. The difference was that the Magi *went to see* while
the experts stayed home! The men of tradition stayed
home, while the really "wise men" found Christ by
following a star.

There are a million reasons why people don't follow
stars. We are restless, we are bothered, but so were the
Magi. But if they had all stayed at home, their restlessness
would never have been quenched. I guess the lesson is that
we have no right to complain about our restlessness if we
are not willing to follow the star inside of us. We have no
reason to complain about our lack of peace if we will not
take on the restlessness of being a pilgrim. We arrive at
peace by following our star. Just follow it! Stop asking if
we have enough faith. Just start walking. God will give us
faith as we journey. *Get going* and you will find Christ.
You will have enough faith because he will be with you as
you journey.

Matthew 2: 13-23   *PATRON SAINT OF THE REAL*

In this short Gospel we hear three times that something was fulfilled that was spoken through the prophets: "Out of Egypt I have called my Son;" "Rachel lamenting her children and would not be comforted;" and "the Messiah should be called a Nazarene." And all this came about through the instrumentality of someone who only did what he was told.

The two messages to Joseph in the Gospel are the same: "Arise and take the Child and his mother and fly into Egypt;" "Arise, and take the Child and his mother and go to the land of Israel." And that is all we hear about Joseph in the whole Gospel. There is very little more in the whole of the Gospel tradition. And yet, this man is the Patron of the whole Church.

This man Joseph is the very first, if you will, of the desert Fathers. He is the first man to live in solitude, simplicity, and silence. He is the continuation of the long and unspoken prophetic tradition in the Old Testament. The names of few of these men have come down to us today, except for Elijah. St. Joseph remains for us the man through whom all the greatest yearnings of all mankind were fulfilled and yet himself accomplished "nothing." He is the patron saint of the power and mystery of interior activity.

You might say that he is the patron saint of the real, the patron saint of the truly simple. He stands there, next to the holy Mother of God, as a constant reminder that our faith and our life of faith is a mystery of each individual heart. No action whatsoever of itself proves either to God or to man who a man really is. It is a mystery of his own heart. Beginning with St. Joseph, God has raised up in the history of the Church people who have done nothing else but live—live in purity, in prayer, in simplicity, and in deep fidelity to the Son of God.

There is a tendency to contrast St. Joseph's life with a life of feverish activity, and to see the former as a condemnation of the latter. But I think he is much too gentle to be a condemnation. He is the kind of person who by his very presence and compassion can quiet troubled hearts. We hear frequently the dictum from the eastern Fathers, "Keep your heart in tranquility and a multitude will find salvation *near* you."

If there is anything to which the Church is called upon today to do, it is to be that kind of reality—a place near which people can find salvation. Maybe this is why Joseph is the patron of the Church. If there is anything that is needed, it is this simple Christ-confidence, a true self-confidence because Christ dwells in us. We don't need to *do* a lot of things. What we need to do is to hear the voice of God and do what needs to be done—a different matter!

After all, it wasn't a small accomplishment to have to care for the Christ Child on a journey to Egypt of about 600 or 700 miles. It took some organizing to find a place to move into, to settle down, to take care of the Mother of God. So it wasn't that Joseph didn't do anything. But whatever he did the emphasis was on being real in the quietness of his heart, in prayer, with the kind of heart that takes love for granted, and trusts.

Silence is the daughter of hope. When we love God enough to take God's love for granted (that is, accept it because it really has been offered), then its reality is too great and too obvious to need proving. Such a hope gives birth to joy.

When we think of this mysterious man, let us hear the Word of God as addressed to us, the Word which he addressed to Joseph: "My friends, be silent. God loves you. My friends, pray. God is with you. My friends, serve.

Then you will reflect God." And if we have the courage to be real as Joseph was, then the Lord can do with us what he wants. Then we will know that even if we never move, or if nothing exteriorly great ever happens, we will know, as Joseph knew, that we have made Christ present to the world.

Matthew 3: 13-17   *HE WHO HIDES*

The manifestation of God is necessarily a hiding of God. If God didn't manifest himself at all we would never know him. We could guess about God, think about him, but we would never know him. And yet, when God reveals himself he also hides himself. When God chose to appear to us he took on a tiny form, became a child, a man, died and rose. All of this is the revelation of God, but also the hiding of God. God is greater than any of his appearances, greater than any of his manifestations.

Our greatest problem is that we demand that God appear on our terms and be sufficiently dramatic about it. In our arrogance we want to be able to say, "This is God." But God does just the opposite. He appears in the very small and ordinary, to remind us constantly of our need of his greatness and mercy. No revelation of God is equal to God. Were God to appear in a great thunderous roar, a bolt of lightning, or wind and fire, we would be so impressed we might worship the wind and fire and say, "This is God." But all those things are so far from God. So God appears in ways that reveal his own inner life, but still leaves us somewhat in mystery.

In the Gospel account there are three mysteries celebrated. The main one is not the manifestation of Christ but of the Trinity: Father, Son, and Holy Spirit. In his baptism, Christ reveals the life he lives: the inner life of

God. Every one of us at baptism had these words addressed to us: "This is my son, my child, my favor rests on him." They are uniquely true of Christ. The greatest glory of the Christian is that he knows God: Father, Son, and Holy Spirit; yet, the greatest pain of a Christian is that he does not know God: Father, Son, and Holy Spirit! So we live in a world in which Baptism and water, Eucharist and bread continue the Incarnation itself: revealing God yet hiding God. Nothing can fully reveal God, except God. Therefore every epiphany leads us to a deeper longing for the vision of God.

The way to God is the way of great humility. Put aside anything that doesn't lead to God. God chose to reveal himself to the Wise Men through a star. There is no comparison between a star and God. There is no comparison between the whole created world and God. If God says to the Wise Men, "Follow that star," then they follow it. If God says of the Son of Man, "This is my Son," then we listen, open up to Christ, and see that he truly is the Son of God. He is the inner expression of God.

"No one has ever seen God, but the only-begotten who lives in the very heart of God has declared him." And so let us take out of our hearts all arrogance, all sensuality, all stupidity, and be attentive to the truly inadequate revelation of God that he gives us. Let us be simple enough to follow the way that he leads. Let us go beyond our puny knowledge to a living knowledge of the Holy Trinity. In the words of the Roman preface: "In the wonder of the Incarnation your eternal Word has brought to the eyes of faith a new and radiant vision of your glory. In him we see our God made visible, and so are caught up in love of the God we cannot see."

The Gospel we are considering is a theophany, a manifestation of God. Every revelation of God imparts a knowledge of God, but also necessarily hides him. There is no way of remedying this until we see him face to face.

However, those who are completely open to the revelation of God truly know him, although in an imperfect way. Those who balk at this revelation, those who don't take it seriously, receive the revelation of God but run the risk of not knowing God. Since every manifestation of God is going to be also a hiding of God, it demands from us great purity of heart if this manifestation is going to shine through us to others.

The greatest, most learned and inspired sermon in the world could be an utterly inadequate revelation of God, whereas a smile, a look of kindness inspired by the Spirit at the right time, could be a much deeper manifestation. Therefore, we can't be arrogant in deciding how we are going to try and reveal God to others. For the great mystery of God, the awesome mystery of God is too much for us. We don't determine who God is and how he will manifest himself through us. He does. The glory of being a Christian, the glory of singing God's praises, is that we know him. We worship the Father of our Lord Jesus Christ in his Spirit. If we pray for one another, maybe we'll learn the humility and the single-mindedness to follow the inadequate revelations of God—the revelations that God chooses—and come to a living knowledge of God.

Matthew 6: 14-21   *FOOTPRINTS OF GOD*

Christian liberty means that most of the things we think are so important are not important at all. If we are alive and love God and love one another and everyone we meet, all the rest of life is mere detail. The rest of life is a mystery, a contact with God. Our life-style: the way we walk, the form of our pilgrimage, is basically not that important.

If there are those who give glory to God by fasting, by not eating meat, and by spending long hours in prayer, may God be praised by such people! May they give him glory and simplicity of heart! And if there are others who eat whatever they find, work hard, or have to sleep long hours and don't have much time for prayer, but who love God and everyone they meet, may God be praised by them! And may they also, in the spirit of simplicity and childhood, give glory to the Lord, who loves everyone and who wills only that we love him!

I think this is the basic message of this Gospel. The needs of our poor bodies are infinite and they'll never make us happy. We're pushed around by so many forces in this world, by so many desires. At bottom, they're all reflections of our need for God. Whether the desire is for water or food or consolation or assurance, they're all symbols of our need for God.

So the advice given to us in the Gospel is not that we are evil, or that the needs of our bodies are evil. These needs are all images. When we're very, very thirsty, we have a tiny image of what is going on deep inside of us. We are thirsty for God. Once in a while, if we are really thirsty or hungry or lonely, and we can feel it, then we have access to a deeper level in us where we're always hungry and thirsty and lonely for God. If we chase the images, we may not find God. God made our bodies, the world, and everything that we often inordinately yearn for. If we chase all those things and try to satisfy all our desires, we get hungrier and thirstier and lonelier, because they're not leading us to God. It is only when our hearts are pure that these desires become sources of joy, because they remind us of how much we miss God.

When our Lord tells us that when we fast we shouldn't look so gloomy about it, it's because in faith we ought to know that we're making our way to God. Our

Lord tells us "where your treasure is, there will be your heart." So what is our treasure? What are we looking for? We're looking for God.

We get all mixed up. We go down every side street we can find. We get bored and tired and frustrated. We back-track. We start over again. All the time we're looking for God. That's where our hearts really are. Deep down we're looking for God. Our heart is like a compass needle. It knows where to turn. The Spirit of God is in our hearts. If we are just quiet and able to listen, we will have a dim idea of where our treasure is.

An old starets used to say that we don't have to rack our brains to grind up some great ideas about God. All we have to do is to start looking for him quietly. And that's our treasure. Every once in a while, like the fellow who found the treasure in a field, we may have to sell everything and take one great "financial risk." And when we do that we find in a deeper way, all over again, our treasure. And then all of creation can speak to us. All the things that reflect God, that shine with God, will become a delight. They become a touch of God, a symbol of God, an image of God, a footprint of God, and we're delighted.

All of us know those things that lead to our peace. How many times we take upon ourselves those things that disturb our peace. Being hungry and thirsty are meant to open our eyes to the deeper hunger within. All the things we want, all the things we yearn for, we see now that they're all really God.

Matthew 6: 22-32   *HE TRUSTED TOO MUCH!*

When we hear this Gospel or read it we can catch something of our Lord's great desire to heal us of our fears. How many times in that one text do we hear the phrase, "don't be anxious"? Can you imagine what it was like to hear our Lord saying "Look at the birds, look at the lilies of the field"? He wasn't trying to construct a whole philosophy of how one should go about providing for one's bodily needs. He was trying to heal something very deep in us: that anxiety by which we live the life of trying to provide for one's bodily needs. He was trying to heal something that is so much a part of our ordinary way of operating: that anxiety by which we try to provide everything for ourselves, and consequently never come to experience that God is our Father who cares for us.

St. Paul, in a much more theological way, is saying the same thing when he says, "Look, the love of God is poured forth in our hearts by the Holy Spirit." All the deepest things we yearn for, the greatest things we pray for, are as nothing compared with what God wants to give us. God is our Father, constantly present to us saying, "Don't be anxious."

Our response is, "Wait a minute, Lord. After all, if nobody ever worked where would all these clothes come from? And if nobody sowed or plowed, where would this food come from?" This is a superficial response. It shows we have misunderstood the intent of the admonition. The great challenge that our Lord is throwing at us is so much deeper, so much more true. We think of so many objections because we don't want to hear the truth.

I suppose, in a way, it would have been necessary to have been there and to have seen our Lord's preoccupation in trying to heal us of this anxiety. We think, "But if I abandoned myself like that, the way Christ says, I might be fooling myself. Perhaps it's not really the way he says. Perhaps I should be doing something else." Perhaps, perhaps, perhaps, perhaps, perhaps, perhaps. We're always afraid of over-trusting. They pay some poor guy $200 to walk across a tight-rope 200 feet off the ground. He risks his life every day for $200. We have God's word, but it isn't enough of a guarantee. Suppose we trusted God too much. Boy, that would be great! Suppose it was written on our tombstone: "Here lies Harry who trusted God too much and starved to death." Poor guy!

Jesus says, "Look at the birds of the air." So, look at the birds. They're busy flying around eating bugs and everything. Look at them. They're not nervous. It's rare you see one of them sitting on a branch looking like he's saying, "Okay, God, where are the bugs?" They're not anxious at all.

Suppose we started trusting God too much. Is it possible that God would let us down for trusting him? If those lilies and birds don't seem to be concerned, why don't we try it? The flowers and the birds don't even know that God is taking care of them. They don't have a mind. They give great glory to God because they're too busy looking for bugs to even think about it. They're not nervous; they're not anxious.

Our Lord wants to heal that anxiety in us. He wants us to know how free he made us so that we're not up-tight. We who don't know where to look for God are fed by God. We who don't know how to pray have our prayers heard before we say them. We who don't know how to provide for ourselves are cared for by God. May we come to be touched by the great mercy of God our Father who cares for us because we are his children.

Matthew 8: 18-27   *NO GUTS, NO GLORY!*

In St. Matthew's Gospel this incident in the life of our Lord, this crossing of the sea which culminates in the healing of a demoniac, begins with two statements about discipleship. One is, "Master, I will follow you wherever you go," to which our Lord replies, "the foxes have holes, the birds their nests, but the son of Man has nowhere to lay his head." The other is a statement by another disciple: "Master, I will follow you, but first let me go home and bury my father," to which our Lord replies, "Let the dead bury the dead. You come and follow me."

In the other synoptic accounts of this story it is placed in another context. St. Mark says explicitly that the disciples took our Lord with them in the boat. Matthew has just discussed what it means to be a disciple, that is, to follow Jesus. He then changes the incident on purpose. Jesus got into the boat and it was the disciples who *followed him*. Those who are to be with Christ, as this incident begins to transpire, are those who followed him.

At once a violent storm came up and the waves were about to swamp the boat. They came to Jesus, who was sleeping, and cried out to him, "Lord save us or we will perish." Mark expresses it more vigorously: "Lord, don't you care if we are going to drown!" Interestingly enough, after Matthew places this plea on the lips of the disciples, he records that our Lord pointed out to them that they were cowards and that they lacked faith. Then, standing up, he exercises the same power over the chaos that we read about in the opening lines of Genesis. The winds and the sea obey him. He speaks and everything is calm.

If we dwell on this Gospel it seems to be full of mysteries. This Lord, who exercises the power of creation over the storm and the chaos, is Jesus, who got into a boat with his disciples following him. And yet, when they cry out to the Lord to be saved, he reprimands their cowardice and lack of faith. Obviously, for Matthew, and not just for subsequent preachers, this boat is the Church, because the Church is the place where the disciples follow Jesus.

If we follow Jesus we can be sure of running into storms! You and I are just tiny fragments and reflections of the Church, and there are storms in us. But there are also storms raging in the whole Church as well, storms which all the skills of navigation can't seem to handle. The waves coming at us are just too big. This has been true every minute of every day since the Church existed. Maybe today we are lucky to be living in a time when it is painfully obvious.

Christianity is not the "in thing" today, nor has it ever been. All the storm waves of ignorance, shortsightedness, and hate are really tossing the ship. As Matthew puts it, we too cry out "Lord, save us!" Our Lord's rebuke is not directed at the prayer but at their lack of faith, their cowardice.

If you never follow Jesus you will never know what a real storm is like. You have to get into the boat. You have to make a choice. The disciples didn't know that the minute they followed Jesus there would be a storm. But we know. We can read the story of our own lives right here in this Gospel. There is nothing wrong with crying out to Christ to calm the storm. But we would be doubly at fault if we were cowards, and if we doubted even as we called out to him.

How many times has our Lord told us to pray? How many times has he said that if we shout long enough he will answer us, even as the judge answered the importunate widow? Jesus is not making believe that the storm does not exist, or that it is some kind of illusion, or that there really is no danger of the ship going down. And both he and we know very well that if we depended only on our own skill or the skill of the Church to get across the lake, the boat would have sunk long ago. What he chides us for is being so filled with fear that we forget with whom we are riding.

I am quite sure that everyone knows what the storm is all about. And we know what it is all about precisely

because we have followed Jesus and are in the boat. It may
be that the very challenge of our faith is to allow ourselves
to experience the full brunt of the storm, in the
confidence that Christ can calm the waves any time he
wants to. It may be that we are supposed to take the risk
of faith and really experience what the storm is, crying out
"Lord, save us" even at the risk of a rebuke.

Suppose we get too scared? Suppose we're like Peter
walking on the water who gets scared and calls out the
very same words as he is sinking? It doesn't matter. Let us
never become so afraid that we're afraid of being corrected
by Christ. There were men on the shore that day who
didn't receive Christ's correction. They didn't receive it
because they just stayed on the shore and didn't follow
him. They had one consolation: they can say that they
were never rebuked by Christ. True, but neither did they
experience the power of this man who calmed the wind
and the raging sea.

Matthew 8: 28-34   *LORD, YOU MAKE US NERVOUS*

I suppose in one sense the most striking part of the
Gospel is the gesture of Jesus by which he cures these two
people and sends a whole herd of swine down into the
lake. But I think if you look closely, you see that the
Gospel is in a way perhaps a reflection of the mystery of
fear, of loneliness, of healing, and of rejection. I am sure
that by now it is common knowledge that when the New
Testament speaks of a demoniac, it needn't be someone
"possessed." It often means someone whose illness is such
that the power of evil, sickness, and corruption of the
human race is dramatically portrayed in this person.
Perhaps it is mental illness, or epilepsy. The grip of evil on
us is dramatically portrayed in someone who is very sick.
(Perhaps that is why we tend to be afraid of such people.)

In St. Mark's Gospel there is only one demoniac, and he was so fierce that no one would pass that way. He lived in a tomb and every once in a while someone tried to catch him; but he broke the chains and ran away. When our Lord asked his name he said, "My name is legion." When the Gospel points out that these demons went into the pigs, it is only to highlight the demons' true nature. For a Jew, anything that had to do with pigs was revolting. The power of our Lord is displayed by the fact that he could dispel these demons and give them over to the pigs.

Can you imagine the purity of heart of our Lord as he confronted this sea of loneliness, fear, and fierceness? By a simple gesture he heals these men. Such a display of the power of wholeness—the power of one removed from these unwholesome drives—so upsets the town's people that they tell Jesus not to come back this way. "Why don't you go back to where you came from? You make us nervous " And he went back another way.

St. Mark says that the man who was cured wanted to go with Jesus. Jesus said: "No, stay here and tell people what happened to you." The Gospel tells us not only what is happening now in the world, or what happened in the time of Christ, it tells us what is happening now in our own lives with Christ. Doesn't the awful power and purity of the presence of Christ sometimes make us nervous? Don't we too feel like saying sometime, "Why don't you go away. Take the next bus out of here. Don't get too close."

In every healing story the mystery is that we are the healed, and the one who can heal others. We are the objects of Christ's power, and we are the bearers of it to others. If we first knew what it was to be healed, we would know what it was that afflicted everyone else. The power and mystery of God is that we don't have to be perfectly

healed before we can heal others. Otherwise there would
be little healing going on!

But what is it that afflicts this man who is so fierce
that no one can go near him? He is a human being. After
Christ has healed him, he is quiet. He is beautiful. When
Christ heals, he doesn't destroy. The awesome thing about
this person is how quiet he is after our Lord healed him.
That amazed people.

In other words, we are healable, we are curable, and
so is the whole human race. It comes down to this: insofar
as we let Jesus cast out from us the drives of fear, anger,
selfishness, fierceness, estrangement, alienation—to that
degree we are able to understand why people live in tombs
and weep and are so fierce that no one can pass their way.

This world is deeply afflicted with demons that make
men so fierce that no one can pass by their way. When
these demons are dispelled, there is a real human being
there, a real person, beautiful. There is no one who is not
beautiful in Jesus Christ. So we are called to chase out
those demons and make people human. Our first task is to
allow ourselves to be healed, to allow ourselves to accept
the gift of purity of heart so that there is nothing to be
afraid of. If we keep our own hearts in peace then it is true
that many will find salvation and healing near us. If we
allow Christ to chase out the drives that push us around,
then we are healed.

If, on the other hand, we are like the people in the
town where this healing presence was too much for them,
we too will be among the lonely and the fierce and the
scared who can still fear other people and through whom
very little healing can come. Let us pray that we may be
open to receive the healing power of Christ. Then we will
glory in our weakness and the power of Christ will abide in
us.

Matthew 9: 1-8 *YES, LORD, I THINK YOU CAN*

I was talking about this Gospel to someone and she said to me, "What was it that our Lord had that people went to him like that? Why did these two blind men cry out like that, "Son of David, have pity on me!"? Why did they bring this man who couldn't speak?"

These two blind men came to Jesus and addressed him by a title full of honor: Son of David. And he turned to them (at least in St. Matthew's Gospel) and said: "Do you believe I can do this?" And they said, "Yes, yes." All right, he touched their eyes and they saw. Then they brought this man to him who couldn't speak and again our Lord loosens his bond. The Pharisees say He is driving out these devils by the forces of evil.

Our Lord did not stop and answer that objection specifically. He said, "Well, if what I do comes from the power of the devil, how about your children when they pray and things happen. Will you say that satan's kingdom is divided against itself?" When this objection is brought up, Matthew at this point in his Gospel ignores it. It does prove something: the power and presence of our Lord is not so compelling that people can't think of objections. And then the story goes on. Our Lord went about teaching in the synagogues about the kingdom of God and healing everyone.

St. Paul, in one of his letters, tells us that when we read the scriptures we get hope because we see all the people who wouldn't give up. They were finally healed by God. This is a consolation to us. Now we can tolerate one another and be friendly with the friendship of Christ toward one another. We are encouraged by the scriptures not to give up, and that is hope.

We see in our Gospel two blind fellows who have not yet received an immediate response to their request. Christ didn't say right away, "Sure, I'll heal you." He said, "Do you really believe I can do this for you?" They had to stop and think a moment: "Do I really think he can do this thing for me?" Then they said "Yes, yes, we think you can do it." Jesus said, "According to your faith, let it be done," and it was done.

Who is Jesus? What was it about him that caused people to approach him like that? First of all, he must have been very approachable. These people were outcasts from society, but evidently they had no trouble in going up to him. Secondly, he was not overpowering or absolutely irresistable. People who didn't want to see continued in their blindness. He is above all compassionate. He goes around teaching and healing.

These stories are meant to give us hope. The healing power of Jesus is present right here and now because he is present. He promised us he would be present and so he is. But his presence and his power, then as now, are not overwhelming. There is no compelling argument that he is present, nor is there irrefutable proof that he can heal. It is a risk. But by the very fact that he is not overpowering, gives us a chance to hope. We are really a lot like the two blind men. The first question we are going to ask ourselves, prompted by the Spirit (though we might think it is a doubt), would be the very question our Lord asks: "Do you really think anything will happen?" "Am I talking to myself? Is it worth praying? Will anything come of it?" These questions are not always exactly doubts; neither are they mere rational, logical processes. It might very well be the Spirit of God prompting us to look into ourselves and see.

Now those two blind men really wanted to be healed. When our Lord said, "Do you think I could do it?" they took a chance and said, "Sure, sure you can do it." This does not signify that they already possessed a perfect faith, but there is a real openness to Christ. "Yes, Christ, I do believe." He says, "OK, that's enough. See." Then they really had faith, and their seeing is contrasted with the unseeing of the Pharisees who say He is doing it in the power of the devil.

What am I trying to say in all this? Well, it has to do with the original question I was asked. What was there so majestic and mysterious and at the same time so approachable, compassionate, and understanding about Christ? It was his personality. It is a fact that he is the Son of the Living God, and that is not a reality that we begin to accept as a clear, well-defined formula, as a guide according to which we must pray. It is a reality to which we open our hearts, a reality which we come to understand more deeply every day. The healing presence of Christ is with everyone of us all the time—in prayer, in mystery, and in one another.

For if we show one another that friendliness which is the friendship of Christ, and tolerate one another, help one another not to give up, then we help one another to answer Christ when we approach Him, "Yes, Lord, I really think you can do it." And we give each other this hope, not by ourselves, but by that openness, that friendliness, that friendship which Christ inspires in each of us.

Matthew 9: 27-35   *ALWAYS ROOM FOR. . . ?*

It's one of the characteristics of St. Matthew's Gospel that he always looks to see what's going on inside somebody when they come up to our Lord. What attitude do they have? And he always highlights that first. It's very important to him and he has a tendency when he tells the story of the various healings that our Lord worked to take

away all the secondary details, so that there's a confronta
tion between Jesus and the person talking to him.

St. Mark, for instance, tells us that it was Peter who
went and told Jesus about his mother-in-law when she was
sick. Matthew leaves all that out, so that when our Lord
enters the house, it's Jesus who sees the woman sick and
Jesus who goes up to her, and there's no intermediary,
there's nobody between those two people. That's a
characteristic of the way Matthew views faith. Another
characteristic is that as Matthew speaks, he describes the
attitude that he sees in the person; then the request of the
person is answered literally. When the leper says, "Lord,
cleanse me," the Lord says, "Yes, I will. Be cleansed." And
he was cleansed. These people wanted their sight and they
got their wish.

Now there's an undertone going through this. After
our Lord has worked this miracle of giving sight to these
two people—after our Lord has taken the spirit of darkness
out of someone so that he speaks and bears witness—the
Pharisees say, "He's doing this by the Prince of Darkness."
At this point in St. Matthew's Gospel, the remark is
ignored. Later on it will be picked up and answered, but
not here. And then comes the summary of our Lord's
whole career: that our Lord went around teaching in the
synagogues, preaching the kingdom and healing. And that's
the end of this particular Gospel reading.

Interesting that we see these two blind men, men who
can't see, calling out to Christ in faith. And the Pharisees
who can "see," blinded themselves. When the Lord
passes—because of who he is—he is as hidden as he is
revealed; it's up to us to see him as he really is. We're never
forced into that. A miracle happens right before our eyes!
We can always say, "Oh no, it's something else, something
I ate, the time of year, and so on. We might not go as far as
the Pharisees who said that it was the work of the devil,

but neither are we forced by the happening to say "It's the Lord's work."

The Son of God is God of God, and Light of Light. He is infinitely mysterious. And the fact that he reveals himself doesn't mean that he loses any of his mystery. We never have a secure hold on God; we're never forced, because God has such a great respect for the freedom he gave us and also because of the very nature of God. The only utterly compelling manifestation of God would be the vision of God face to face with no intermediary whatsoever. But that would be the end of history because no one could see God and live.

If God were to burst right now into our room, the very vision of God would transform us and we wouldn't be living in this world. We wouldn't be living in history anymore. History would be over, at least for us. And it would be over for the whole world, depending on how God revealed himself. But God is not going to do that. God is making history. God made human life. This is the meeting place where God works in mystery, and man grows in love. So God is not going to do that.

Like those two blind men we call out, "Son of David, have mercy on us." Matthew tells the same story twice. These two blind men here he mentions again in the incident where the crowd tells the two to "be quiet! You are ruining this whole beautiful teaching experience." The Lord steps up and says, "Let those two fellows come forward." During this whole procession there are only two guys with faith, and they can't even physically see.

So there's quite a contrast between blindness and sight. The blind will see, as Isaiah prophesied, and as the Lord himself will point out very shortly in Matthew's Gospel. When John's disciples ask him, "Who are you?" the Lord says, "Go and tell John what you see. The lame walk, the blind see, the dead are raised to life." Already blind, these two men see because they call out. They don't even know exactly in which direction Jesus is. They can only vaguely determine his whereabouts. And they cried out, "Jesus, Son of David, have mercy on us."

Jesus is the Son of David. Jesus has flesh and blood. The manifestation of Jesus Christ, as he walked around, as he died and rose, was not so compelling that everybody just *had* to follow him. The signs of God are attractions to something deeper; the knowledge of God which is beyond all signs and all manifestations and all experience and all knowledge, requires deeper vision.

He to whom we appeal is a man, the Son of David, Messiah, a human being, Son of God. The depth of our heart tells us that, and then we ask for sight. These two blind men when they were healed followed him and became his disciples. The Lord's love forced them to call out, but their call was in faith.

When the Christian tradition calls baptism the "enlightenment," it is usually thinking of this Gospel. Every day we are called upon to renew that baptism, that enlightenment. Every day we are in some kind of blindness. Maybe our first cry is one of sheer desperation. There is simply no one else to turn to. And as we call out we are rewarded, not perhaps immediately with sight, but with a real confrontation with Jesus. We might be so petrified that our response is muffled. It doesn't matter. "Lord, I believe. Help my unbelief."

The Gospel is not given to us simply to be read. These things were not written down so that we would have edifying stories to think about. Jesus is present in his Word. It contains a power which can be let loose at this very moment if we have the faith to call out. And as we call out, let us pray not only for our own healing, but like these two blind men, let us say, "Have mercy on *us*." Let us pray for all the world, that the Lord will heal and give sight to all men.

Matthew 14: 22-34   *LEANING ON GOD*

Whenever St. Matthew tells stories about the disciples and about that lake in Galilee, there are always overtones about the life of the Church.

In this incident, which is just after the multiplication of the loaves and fishes, Jesus goes up to the mountain to pray by himself. Then the disciples see him walking on the water. St. Peter says, "Lord, if that's you out there, bid me come to you." And Jesus said, "Alright, come." So Peter got out of the boat and started to walk on the water. And then he looked around and saw what he was doing, and he was afraid. At once Jesus took him, just as he started to sink, and brought him back into the boat. He said to him, "Why did you doubt, O you of little faith?"

Because Peter got out of the boat and walked on the water, he knew that the Lord had power to let him do such a thing. It was no longer a nice, abstract question; it was now a faith experience. In this he is a symbol of what faith is really all about. The truth of Jesus Christ and the truth of God's word is not a thing we know by merely thinking about it. We can only really know it by doing it.

Some truths we can know just with our heads, such as two and two are four. Other truths we can see, such as the sun coming up in the morning. But there are certain truths about God that we can only know by going halfway to meet them.

Peter's walking on the water is a good example of what the Bible means by truth. Truth is solid, it doesn't move, doesn't vanish. How are we going to know if God is true or not? By leaning on him. See if he is solid. Lean

over so far on God that if he is not going to hold you up
you are going to fall flat on your face. Then you will know
that God can uphold you, that he is true.

How many times in our lives are we challenged like
Peter was? Usually we have a lot more "cool" than Peter.
Few of us would say, "Is that you out there, Lord? I'll be
out right away." NO, usually we are a lot cooler. We don't
want to make a fool of ourselves. We might say, "If James
goes, I'll go!" Or we say, "Lord, how do I know that I can
walk on water?" He says, "You don't!" "How will I
know?" "By walking." "But Lord, I'm afraid." "I know."
But even God can't prove to us that he is trustworthy, that
he is true, by simply giving us an argument. Even God
can't do that. We have to meet him halfway.

I could prove to you that the wall next to you would
hold up if you leaned against it. But until you actually
leaned against it you would still have a doubt. Biblically
that is exactly what the trueness of God means. It means
that you can lean on him, that you can put your weight on
him and you won't collapse.

It may concern only a tiny movement of our heart
during the day. It may be a big decision in life. It could be
anything. But what a great thing it is to go ahead even
when we're scared and we know that we'll probably sink in
a few minutes. Our Lord never said, "Don't be afraid to
walk on the water." He just said, "Come."

So this Gospel is the Gospel of faith. Is the Lord
saying to you today, "Come, walk?" "But Lord, I'm
scared." "I know you're scared." "Can't you give me any
guarantees?" "What guarantees can I give you but my
word. If you don't walk on the water you'll never know if
I'm true or not. So walk." "Suppose I sink?" "Why do you
think I'm standing right here? I'll pick you up. Don't
worry about that. That's beside the point. If you start to
sink, I'll pick you up. Walk."

We can laugh at Peter's impetuosity, but maybe we should pray for just a little bit of it. It would be great to be able to leap out of the boat even before we knew what happened. If we sit around in that boat, thinking, thinking, thinking, we'll never experience the truthfulness of God.

Matthew 18: 21-35   *LOVE DOESN'T KEEP SCORE*

In some ways this is the easiest Gospel to talk about and in another way it is the hardest, because the lesson is so obvious. In one sense there is nothing to draw out or explain. The last line of our Lord sums up completely the whole message of the parable. Obviously the great king is God, and the person who owes this king several million dollars is obviously you and I. And the fellow who owes us about $100, that is our brother. Unless we forgive these little debts between one another, our Father will not ratify the debt that is already forgiven us. There is really nothing else to say.

The parable is introduced in the Gospel of St. Matthew with the question of Peter, "How many times shall my brother sin against me and I forgive him?" And our Lord answers, "Seventy times seven," that is, without count. You don't stop forgiving. Forgiveness isn't a thing you measure. Either you have it and always forgive, or you don't have it and don't forgive.

Interestingly enough, both the man forgiven by the great king, and the fellow-servant, pleaded in exactly the same terms for mercy, and the word they used is "be patient with me." Indeed, the man in debt said, "I will pay you back in full," but obviously he never could do that. Still, the king writes off the debt. The servant says, "Be patient with me." It is the same word which St. Paul used when he said, "Love is patient."

There is a certain great-souledness about love. It keeps no score of wrongs. The truth of the matter is obvious. That is why we are forgiven by God. The forgiveness of our brother is not, as it were, a certain contract or even an imitation of God. It is that act by which we allow the power of Christ to be manifested to one another within a human dimension. We give it a full human existence. Whom do I forgive? Anybody who needs it. Sometimes long before they ask for it. The very fact that someone is forgiven may be the grace, may be the light that enables them to ask for it. When we were *still sinners*, Christ died for us.

Our Lord said, "As often as you do these things to the least of my brethren, you do it to me." Do you ever think that you are forgiving Christ? Do you ever think of encouraging Christ, the Christ who suffered, who is weighed down, who is lonely in his flesh right now? If it is true that no one suffers alone, anyone who forgives is also ministering to Christ who suffers in each of his members.

There can be other objects of our forgiveness besides individuals. What about forgiving our culture which we think in so many ways is harmful to people? What about forgiving bishops or pastors whom we don't think are moving fast enough to implement the Vatican Council? What about forgiving the Fathers at the Council of Trent, if we think they are responsible for the bind we are in presently? What about forgiving our government, our city councils, our school boards if we are holding a grudge against them? What about forgiving all those who really are persecuting the Body of Christ in so many places around the world? Each one of these grudges causes a wound in our hearts which has to be removed through forgiveness.

And forgiveness is not merely the absence of blame, a sort of negative not fighting back. "Live and let live" I always say! No. Forgiveness is a positive act of love. We ourselves pray that God will give us his Holy Spirit for the remission of our sins. We expect God to act positively in our regard. When God forgives it is not a question of simply no longer considering us guilty. When God forgives he gives life. How many times do we "forgive" by simply no longer demanding retribution? And then we consider ourselves quite magnanimous and broad-minded. How many times, on the other hand, do we give our love? How often is our forgiveness a positive thing? If it isn't, it isn't Christian forgiveness. It isn't what God has done for us.

Forgiveness means that we have to give something, not merely refrain from condemnation. Forgiveness is this act of patience spoken of in the Gospel. It is a magnanimous act which imitates the act of God. Forgiveness, you will remember, is somehow proper only to God. "Who can forgive sins but God alone?" When a Christian shares in forgiveness he somehow approaches very closely the perfection of the Father to which Jesus said we are called.

Sometimes we may look inside our hearts and see no condemnation there of anyone. But can we look in there and see positive forgiveness, positive patience with those who have wronged us or who we think have wronged us? One of the reasons why we pray for the parousia is precisely so that all these emotions of anger and hostility which we cannot now bring completely within the power of the resurrection may finally disappear, and we can live totally, as totally as Christ does. The reality of Christ is as present now as our capacity to forgive those who stand in need of forgiveness. Let us not wait until they ask or approach us. Let us not merely refuse to condemn. Let us do what Christ did for us. *When we were sinners* he died for us.

What this Gospel is saying to us is that we are called to
live a paradox, we are called to be poor so that others
might be rich. This is meant first of all in a very literal
sense. We are called to have less, so that we can give to
others. But most deeply, we are called to go to God so that
we can be present to all our brothers and sisters. The man
went away sad because he had great possessions.
Sometimes we're sad because we have great possessions,
because they give us a certain status in the world and to
move toward God is to be poor and have nothing. We are
sad because following God might mean being helpless in
making our way in the world.

This Gospel and the words of our Lord that follow it
even surprised the disciples. They were astonished, and
they said: "Well, who can be saved then?" Our Lord said
(after a fashion), "Look, that's none of your business.
That's not what I'm talking about. With men this is
impossible, with God everything is possible. God loves all
of his children—rich, poor, sick, strong, everybody. That's
not the problem. I'm saying something else. Don't reduce
it to money and clothes. Of course those things are
important, but don't put the problem in that context.
Listen to me. I'm saying something else. I'm saying that
when you're poor, you can heal."

In St. Mark's Gospel, when our Lord sends out the
disciples, he tells them to carry nothing at all. He says right
after that, "Now lay your hands on the sick and heal them.
Preach the good news."

The mystery of this poverty is that we have to allow
ourselves to move toward God and be lonely on God's
terms, if we want to be present to everyone as Christ is
present. In this present chapter 19 of Matthew we find
both the doctrines on celibacy and the doctrines on

poverty which were developed by the early Church in the apostolic life. We can still hear the disciples saying, "My gosh, if having money means you don't get saved, then who's going to be saved?"

The paradox is that when we're poor we can enrich. How, if we have nothing to give? When we have nothing to give we are caught up by the Spirit of God, and it becomes obvious to the whole world that God is present in our lives, that he loves his children, that he makes his sun to shine on everyone.

But we continue to argue:

"Lord, I have nothing." "That's the way I want you." "But who can be saved?" "It's a silly question and none of your business. The Father who sent me to die and pour out my blood for everyone is a Father who is going to keep accounts in a ledger book? Never. Never. If you want to know the way my Father loves this world, come, follow me. Then you'll know. If you want to know how powerfully God wants to heal this world, then have nothing and you'll know."

"But Lord, what's the connection between having nothing and healing?"

"Why don't you try it and find out? Why don't you try it and find out? Why make me stand here and give you a long dissertation that you don't understand anyway? Why don't you do it? Just follow me, move with me. Move. Now."

The poverty to which our Lord calls us is the poverty that he had. "He, though he was rich, became poor so that we could be rich." "Drop everything and follow me. Move."

We're sad because we have great possessions. Great possessions? What have we got? "I've got four million dollars." Someone who carries nothing in his heart and through whom the Spirit of God can blow freely, why, such a person can create more joy and real happiness with a mere smile than all the money in the world. Such a person can heal more deeply and forever by crying than all the hospitals in the world. Poverty is paradise because it's real. The poverty in which we seek to find out how well we're doing isn't poverty. The poverty we have when we follow Jesus is paradise and true joy.

So losing everything we become as perfect as God and just as rich. If the Lord speaks to us, let us answer, quickly. When the Lord shows us that we have nothing, then let's be proud. Because at that moment we are beginning to be perfect as our Father is perfect, and our love is beginning to have no barriers.

Matthew 20: 1-16   *REJOICING IN GOD'S MERCY*

In some ways it is difficult to determine what the actual situation of this parable was in our Lord's own life. Most probably he gave it as a defense for his associations with the strangest people. Whenever he went anywhere, or stayed anywhere, he seemed to hang around with the little guys: shop keepers, tax collectors, even prostitutes. The Pharisees were shocked. Such people with whom Christ associated were sinners. They could not possibly be keeping all the laws and therefore were not pleasing to God. How dare this man associate with such as these and even promise them salvation! The Pharisees were not only shocked, they were angry. Think of all the effort they expended in being sure they were pleasing to God. After all, it wasn't easy to be a Pharisee and keep all those laws!

This parable is meant to portray the liberality of God. It shows God paying out to each man according to *His* will. It upsets you when you see someone being paid as much as you are, despite the fact that you have kept the law all your life, and apparently the other person hasn't. The Church has always treasured this parable because it sees in it the image of itself. Like those fellows who got to work about four o'clock, just before the whistle blew at five, the early Christians saw themselves as those who had been called at the last minute of history to share in God's kingdom.

But now it may be that the situation is reversed. How many of us feel like the men who came early in the morning and worked all day, only to see the latecomers get the same pay? Our Lord's reply is the same: "Are you envious because I am generous?"

In this reply we have, as it were, the key to Christian freedom, if we can only understand it. If by our Christian lives we are looking for something like more money, we're wasting our time. We may receive a reward for our lives, but not because we deserve it. Some guy who is a Communist may slide home at the last minute. Will we be able to say, "Isn't that beautiful! Isn't that marvelous!" It is the mystery of the liberality of God.

Our relationship to God is not a matter of daily wages. It is the privilege of knowing how much he loves us. It is only out of such an experience of the liberality of God that a Christian can preach the Gospel. Christian preaching is not a matter of going around trying to get everyone to work all day for God. It is a witness, a simple witness to the mercy and liberality of God.

We are not Christians because somehow we have merited it and worked harder at it than others. It is a matter of the mercy of God. A real Christian is not someone who works all day hoping that God will notice and give him a raise. It is someone who spends himself because he loves Christ.

If some guy gets away with the same pay as you for only an hour's work, that's terrific. Then you may be tempted to start working earlier and to lay off in the afternoon, hoping to get hired at the last hour. You may even succeed—but don't think you're a Christian. A Christian does not try consciously to pull this off. The Christian is someone who works all day as hard as he can, realizing all the while that maybe from the purity of his own love there may result the great mercy of God to someone who may receive the same reward he does for less work.

When we finally understand that we are all pagans except for the mercy of God, then we will be free. If we try to imagine ourselves as somehow better than others, if we look for some sort of spiritual poise, if we look for some rational explanation as to why we were hired early, we doom ourselves to frustration, and we undermine the very radiance and joy of our witness for Christ. Then we're just some guy who was standing close to the door of the hiring hall and managed to get called early.

The mercy of God! This hits deeply in our hearts because no matter how we look at it it seems that those guys who worked all day got gypped. That's because we don't understand the mercy of God or the mystery of his love. The fact is that God is God. Whether our problems get answered or not, God is God. He can never be simply someone we plug into to strengthen our wills and who helps us work for a greater salary. We are all beggars. Our joy and our security come from the mercy of God. There is nothing more certain in all the world. When we realize this, we are able to show God to others, because we accept them as God accepted us. We are free when we realize this, and then, because we are free, we can work all day in the vineyard—not for a raise in pay but because we're in love with Jesus Christ. Only this truly sets us free. Only this will allow us to manifest to others something of the mercy of God.

Matthew 22: 2-14   *MARY WAS GOD'S IDEA*

If there is one key word which sums up the attitude that our Lord is looking for as he tells this parable, I suppose the word could be "humility." As our Lord first told the parable it was to make the people realize that the kingdom of God was breaking right in on them while he was speaking. As the Gospel writers continue to tell this story, they make present to us the fact of the Kingdom of God.

There was an interesting description of those who didn't come: they were too busy. Some went their way, one to his farm, another to his merchandise. Some laid hands on the master's servants and killed them. Finally the master sent the servants out to the crossroads of the town and said, "Bring in anybody you can find." That's us.

This is a parable about the Church. We are not the ones who were originally invited. We are the ones who were dragged in. This theme applies in many places in the Gospels: "Many are called, but I could find only a few when I went out to choose them."

What determines God's choice? He chooses us. Why are certain people at the banquet and not others? Perhaps because they are hungry and accept the invitation. Perhaps because they were lucky enough to be in a position where they knew they were hard up. So, they were lucky enough to turn up at the meal.

Mary is a good example of this kind of humility. How many times have we heard her humility praised? We say she was humble and all generations will call her blessed, as though it were some virtue, as though it was something she "practised." Of all the persons coming in from the highways, she is the perfect example. She was born without original sin, but she too lives by the mercy of God. It is in this she finds her joy, because she lives in the truth.

Sometimes we feel like saying to her, "Look, what do you know about hard times? My nerves are shot. But you were immaculately conceived." She might have answered: "If God had wanted me to be the worst prostitute, the biggest sinner that He could save, that would have been fine for me. Being born immaculate was God's idea."

Do we understand? She understands better than any other creature that she doesn't have a dime. She knows the truth. Being immaculately conceived, existing at all, being Mother of God, Queen of heaven—all that was God's idea.

How is it then that realizing this doesn't make us all quietists? If humility is truth, why don't we just allow God to act? Jesus Christ died for this world, and do you think he doesn't know what a mess it's in? Why don't we just ask for humility and sit back and wait for God to act?

Some of the saints have said that humility is a greater gift than the gift of prayer, and we receive both from God. It is a painful gift to receive simply because we don't know what it is. And the paradox is that the humblest people know what true joy is. They are self-assured and peaceful because they live in the truth and the truth makes them free. The sign of original sin is that the truth still scares us. The very thing we're made for scares us!

A devotion to Mary can help remove in us that awful, agonizing lesson of humility. It's a hard gift to receive, and we're scared until we finally possess it. Somehow Mary has the capacity to make things human, gentle and true. I guess what we really mean is that Mary is true. Philosophers say that beauty is a radiant dimension of truth. It is that extra something about truth that makes it shine.

That's what the holy Mother of God does—she shines. I suppose there are lots of people who have difficulties with devotion to Mary. They think she is an obstacle to their direct way to God. The Mother of God is first and foremost a holy Christian woman who worked daily and had a heck of a time understanding what was going on. She stood at the foot of the Cross and finally went to heaven. Sometime in prayer ask her if she is an obstacle to your life with God. She'll help you to sort it all out.

One sign of humility is to accept going to the banquet. Perfect humility is not forgetting that you were dragged out of the gutter. Then truth shines, and people will be able to see the gentle radiance of the truth, as we can see it in Mary.

Matthew 22: 1-14   *SORRY, NOT INTERESTED*

In some ways this Gospel is a preacher's paradise. St. Matthew is applying the first part of the parable with part of another parable, and ending with the phrase he uses a few times in his Gospel—"many are called but few are chosen." The first part of the parable has to do with our Lord's words about the kingdom of heaven. Those who were first invited weren't interested and the king instead sends out to the country roads to bring people in from the highways and byways, street corners and drugstores. That's us. We are the riff-raff, and the people who weren't interested were the friends of the king.

Now the king comes in to see the guests. It was an ancient sign of hospitality to come in and see the guests, but not eat with them. When he saw the man without a wedding garment, he asked him about it. He said nothing and was thrown out, not just outside the door, but outside "where there is weeping and gnashing of teeth," for "many are called but few are chosen."

There has been a lot of speculation on the wedding garment. What do the riff-raff need to be able to stay at he party? St. Matthew doesn't say. St. John Chrysostom and the early Fathers picked up what was apt for their people, and every age has to do the same.

There are two difficulties: we forget that we are riff-raff, that we were dragged off the streets and have no strict right to the party, and secondly, we tend to take the invitation for granted. Like the friends of the king who were originally invited, we also tend to be "uninterested."

And what is it not to have a wedding garment? It's not to do what we know God wants of us. At this moment each one of us knows what God wants of us: more forgiving, more trusting, more faith, more purity of mind and body. There's something that God wants of us now, and that willingness to respond to this call of God is our wedding garment. The danger is that we don't remain "interested" in going to the banquet. That's what disqualified the others. Each was too busy with other things; they couldn't get over-excited about the party.

The beatitudes speak about the poor, the meek, the pure of heart, those who suffer persecution. Maybe we have to remain interested in these qualities of life to stay at the banquet. Blessedness is life. Blessed are those who are at the wedding feast of the Lamb. Not to ignore the invitation we must remain open to the Holy Spirit. We don't ignore the Spirit's invitations.

So this Gospel, like the whole Gospel, is a decision story. Make up your mind, do you want to come or not? Are you interested or not? Do you really want to be a Christian? The greatest danger is simply ignoring the invitation.

"But," you may say, "I was invited in, I was dragged in, forced to come." This isn't the time for logic and mathematics. It's not a matter of being among the first invited or the group dragged in off the streets. It's a question of being interested. There is no status symbol attached to either the first or the second group. *The* status symbol in God's eyes, the only one that really matters, is to be interested in coming to the banquet. If we only understood what the banquet was, we wouldn't really care how we got there!

Matthew 24: 1-34   *PAROUSIA: BEGINNING OF THE END*

There are many reasons why this text is surrounded in such great mystery. One reason is simply the images that are used here. They are a mosaic of texts from the Old Testament. Some of them you will recognize: the Son of Man coming on clouds to receive power and glory; the transformation of the cosmos; Zechariah's description, expanded to include the powers of the nations looking upon the Son of Man and being stricken with sorrow.

The second reason for the mysteriousness of this passage is the fact that the reality in question is beyond human experience; there is no way to speak about it except in symbols. What is the topic of concern? The End-time. But what is the end?

There is an end to mankind's period of waiting to be reconciled with God. This power of reconciliation was not in the world historically. Now the passion, death, and resurrection of our Lord mark the end-time. Man is no longer waiting for reconciliation.

Then, of course, there is the end of each man's life. This repeats the whole history of the cycle of the cosmos.

Finally, there is *THE END*, the definitive manifestation of God which we call the parousia, the coming of Christ. The factors which go to make up this *END* are present now but not fully manifest. Our Lord invites us to look at the signs of the times. "You see when a tree blossoms." Thus also, there is one indication after another that, like the signs in nature, reveal to us what is going on around us, the true situation; so there will be signs of the End.

It's quite an immense task to try and explain this Gospel because there are so many facets to it. One, perhaps, which we can particularly pray and think about is Jesus' statement, "There will be many who will come in my name saying, 'I am the Christ,' and they will lead many astray." Many will come who are false messiahs and false prophets, and they will do great things in order to deceive others.

What Christ is revealing to us is that the parousia or human death are not events which fall from the sky. Rather, his words reveal to us the very depths of what is; he manifests what is going on right now. Such events as human death, for example, reveal both the transitoriness of things and what is truly valuable and permanent about the present.

If then we wish to manifest Christ so that there can be, as it were, a parousia right now, then we need not look here or there, we need not go into the desert or into the house. The kingdom of heaven is within you, it is among you. You look here and there for signs, and the kingdom of heaven is already among you. If we can be faithful to who we really are, if we can accept the fact of the *END*—the end of all our petty little ideas, all that we build upon—and accept the destruction of "our world" which comes with the acceptance of Jesus, then we see the deep meaning of what is already present—the kingdom.

We know the Son of Man appears like a flash of light that brightens the sky and scatters the darkness of the world and within ourselves. This glimpse of the reality of the Son of Man is faith. Yes, like a flash of lightning it comes. We see, and it goes. But the memory of its vision remains. We have truly seen what surrounds us, even though once again it is shrouded in darkness.

There is no use retreating into a primitive idea of history and science. If we want to accept the reality of THE END, the definitive reality of Jesus Christ, we will not be afraid to accept responsibility for the present. We are not waiting around for the Messiah. We accept his presence, though in mystery. It is thus that the world can know the reality and the presence of that act of God which gives consistency and meaning to human life. If we do not base our own existence on the fact of the risen Christ, people will call us false prophets and false messiahs—and they will be right! The problem is that we fear this event so greatly because there are so many things we cling to and because we instinctively see that the things we try to build our lives upon will vanish. If we lived the real message of the Gospel, the ultimate meaning, the parousia, would be for us a lightning flash. We would rejoice because the world would see reflected in us a bit of that light. Men would see the real meaning of existence on this earth.

This is the history of the Church recapitulated. This is the time for us to accept the responsibility for being the Church. Let us not let the world live in darkness and confusion. Let us really be human and allow the world to see the compassion, the kindness, the reality of Christ in our lives. Let our faith be the lamps that give light to all in the house of the world.

This teaching of our Lord doesn't really need a commentary; it's painfully clear. Our Lord doesn't make any subtle theological distinctions whatsoever. He says quite bluntly, "If you did it to anybody, you did it to me, and if you omitted doing it to anybody, you have omitted doing it to me." Now, the people were surprised, not only the bad guys but the good guys too. They said, "Lord, when did we see you and help or not help you?" Everybody was surprised.

Our Lord did not tell us this story to surprise us. He told it so that when we come before him we will not *be* surprised! He tells us now what the issues are, and we know. There is a great mystery here: the union, the identity, between Jesus and everybody on the globe. Our Lord does not in any way water down his statements: "What you do to anybody you do to me." No great distinctions, no complicated subtleties. It's clear, it's a mystery, and for those with faith, it's a great consolation. When the Little Flower couldn't pray sometimes she would go and serve one of her sisters. She would rest content that in that service she was contacting Christ.

We are always in danger of making man a substitute for God. The Church can very easily become a sort of supersocial agency for man in the name of the Gospel. It's true, Jesus doesn't make any distinctions, but somehow *knowing the truth* about this mystery of his presence in others should make us different. When we feed, clothe, visit anybody, we touch Christ. That should give us a kind of reverence about man, even fill us with awe. This is more than being a social agency.

Food and clothing are often sent to people in distress areas around the world. Many people will be surprised one day when Jesus tells them that they were really helping him. But we are not supposed to be surprised, because even now we *know* the mystery of the presence of Jesus. We know something that we can't put into words. We know that in opening our hearts in a movement of the Spirit, we touch God. This is what our Lord said.

There are certain moral consequences which flow from this knowledge that we have. It means that we cannot serve anybody because it makes us feel good. Neither can we move in and "impose" our "help" on people because we think that is what they need. St. Vincent de Paul said that we should pray that the poor "forgive us our gifts." He knew better than anyone else the mixed motives that can attend our giving.

So what am I saying? That we must be constantly tied up in knots when we come across people in need, wondering, if we act or don't act, what Jesus will say about the whole thing? No. Jesus has come to make us free. He knows that deep down we're all looking for God. He is simply telling us of the mystery of God's presence which is always very close to us. When you help somebody, you touch God. He is simply and beautifully revealing to us one of the deepest mysteries of our whole existence. "If you give to someone, you give to me." We are the ones who get all tied up in knots about it. Jesus says that we need not ever be completely alone. We need only to move one tiny step to serve someone else, and we touch God.

Matthew 28: 16-20   *THE FAMILY LIFE OF GOD*

These are the last words according to the Gospel of St. Matthew. They are the last instructions of our Lord before he ascends to his Father. The risen Lord envelops, as it were, this mysterious family of the Trinity. First there is the promise of the declaration that all the authority in heaven and earth is given to him. This is the risen Lord, the Lord of all the universe, the man Jesus, now glorious with the power of his Father.

Then there follows the instruction to teach and to baptize and finally the promise again of the risen Lord, "Behold I am with you even until the end of the world." I am with *you*, which is in the plural. I am with you as my little flock, you with whom I am whenever two or three of you are gathered in my name.

Encircled by this mystery of the risen Christ is the instruction that this baptism should be done in the name of the Father, Son, and Holy Spirit. The name of God is the expression of who God is. If we really understand somewhat of what we are saying when we say, "Glory be to the Father, and to the Son, and to the Holy Spirit," God is present. God is present in his name. God is present not because the words are magical but because someone who means what he says as he says the name of God makes God present. The name of God ultimately turns out to be Father, Son, and Holy Spirit.

We are told in this Gospel to make disciples through the sacraments. Disciples to what? A doctrine? To a formula? No. We are supposed to baptize people into the Father, Son, and Holy Spirit. God's profound mystery is that within the very life of God there are three persons, and they are all precisely that because they are concerned with the other Two. Someone has said that they are a "subsisting altruism." A person is what he is because he is completely concerned with the other.

Now that is the kind of life to which we are called. The reason why Christ can promise to be with us to the end of the world is because we are drawn into this life and we mirror and reflect it in his Name. The life we are drawn into is a family life, a community life. If you ever wandered for years and had a family take you in, then you might know what heaven is going to be like. . .to be drawn into the family life of God and there to see that we are indeed the children of God. You reflect the Father and kiss him in the Spirit. The Father who sees himself in his Son, the Father and Son who embrace one another in an act of love, a gift from and to one another which is so great that it is another Person. This is the life of God in which it is our destiny to share.

We would never know about this life if it weren't for the mystery of the risen Christ. As we see Jesus pray to his Father, we begin to understand that we have a Father. As we see Jesus promise the Spirit, we wait for the Spirit of Christ. As this reality of the Spirit takes place within us, we begin to realize that it is God.

The name of God is Love. The name of God is Father, Son, and Holy Spirit, and insofar as we allow ourselves to be caught up in that life, to hear the murmur of water within ourselves which is, as St. Ignatius said, "the call to come to the Father," we are on the way to eternal life. Insofar as we allow the flame of life to permeate us, to burn in us and reflect in us all concern for the other, we know God. Insofar as we love, insofar as we can go out of ourselves to another, we know God . . .because God is love.

Mark 1: 14-20   *HEARING THE NEW SONG*

The Pope has asked all of the holy people of God to beseech God for vocations. A vocation is a very mysterious thing. It is a call to go. Every Christian receives that call in Christ at baptism. The full fruition of that call, the full meaning of that voice of Christ the Shepherd, will only be known when the fullness of the Body of Christ will have been achieved and all those who have heard the voice of the Shepherd are somehow bound together into Christ, knowing the Father and singing his praises.

We speak of vocations and we mean usually that special charism by which people begin to live now that kind of life which will characterize the whole Church forever. But what we're really praying for is that every man on this globe, every Christian, will realize that call, will really hear the voice of Christ, that voice which is the source of joy and which is the melody of the new song which each person is supposed to sing. So as we pray for vocations, we are praying that every Christian hear the voice of Christ, because in this voice Christ himself is present.

The full fruition of a vocation is the knowledge of Christ which is like Christ's knowledge of the Father. Now this knowledge is a union based on love, and it is lived out as Christ lived out his knowledge of the Father. "My meat is to do the will of my Father."

God has only one plan, only one will, for the salvation of mankind. The mystery of a vocation is not a matter of trying to find the decision of some great cosmic organizer, but to find out how God wants us to live now the one vocation of Christ, so that the whole Body of Christ can be built up. All of us know the mystery of what this vocation is.

If anyone said to us, "Do you hear the voice of Christ?" we'd probably say no, and feel somewhat embarrassed. We have heard it though, that is why we are Christians. We heard the voice of Christ because we were baptized. His Spirit is in us calling us to the Father. We're praying now that all of God's people be able to hear more clearly the voice of Christ and respond more deeply to what it means to have a vocation.

"Christ suffered for us, leaving you an example, that you should follow in his steps. For you were straying like sheep, but have now turned back to the Shepherd and Bishop of your souls."

We want all those who are young, whose life has just begun, to hear deeply the voice of Christ, so that whatever plan Christ has is embodied in this or that particular person, and in whatever historical way he is to live out his life. Vocation is that milieu in which we live out the whole plan of Christ acting in this environment. Every vocation is the same: It is the way we live out this plan of Christ.

The whole Church of Christ has to hear his voice. Since we are the Church we are praying for ourselves. We daily hear the voice of Christ, but we are praying that the People of God hear the voice. We are asking Jesus Christ to draw us more deeply to himself. We are asking Jesus Christ to give us this knowledge of himself which is a union based on love in a deep fidelity to the one plan of God. We are praying that God's will be done—not that God's will be understood, or simply glanced at—but that God's will be *done*.

There is only one will of God, one flock for eternity, one Christ. All this is caught up somehow in the mystery of the will of God. That gentle voice of Christ which comes to our ears little by little will never be fully understood until we see Christ, until we see the Father. That's the meaning of vocation. We needn't dwell on it; we know about it.

We are praying to Christ to let his voice resound in the Church and to let his Holy Spirit so open the souls of the People of God that they hear it and follow it so that the will of God can be done. It is the will of him who loved us so much that he sent his only-Begotten Son to dwell with us and to suffer and die for us on the cross.

This is the will of God, that men be so united to God that they be one. When the Vicar of Christ asks us to pray, it is not just a little order, a little something to pray about. It is the voice of Jesus Christ saying, "Ask anything in my name and I will give it to you." So we should pray today that all the holy People of God hear the Shepherd, that the will of God and all the beautiful, marvelous manifestations of the will of God in the human Church be done. We know how greatly God loves us, and we know that if the will of God is done, there will be given to mankind a happiness beyond anything we can imagine. So let us pray that God's will be done in all the young of the world who have yet to choose that aspect of the will of God. Let us pray that they hear the voice of Christ, telling them what he has done for them. "I came that they may have life. . .and that their joy may be full."

But we are praying also for priests, religious, and married people. We are praying for ourselves, that Christ's voice resound in the will of God, and that his beautiful voice may be heard—and we may know God as he knows us.

Mark 2: 1-12   *ON CARRYING EACH OTHER*

This Gospel is meant to encourage us by showing us the great power we have. It is meant to let us know that there is no sin that the Lord cannot forgive. The Son of Man has power on earth to forgive sin. Secondly, it is meant to let us know what great power and responsibility we have: we too have the power, in Christ, to let loose on the earth the dynamism and reality of forgiveness. We have the power and responsibility to bring others to Christ.

This man couldn't walk, and four others brought him there. This story, like the story of the people who were carrying the dead widow's son of Naim, is meant to let us know how powerful we are as Church. Those we bring to Christ for healing, really receive it. It is up to us to carry our brothers and sisters to the Lord.

It's faith which purifies our hearts. Faith which lets us shed our sins. Faith that makes our whole being yearn for God as this man yearned to see and have Jesus touch him. The Son of Man has forgiven sins and his light has begun to spark in us. In his light we too are able to forgive each other.

St. Paul said that the law of Christ consists in carrying each other's burdens. Sometimes the burden is the whole person! We must carry to the Lord all those who are finding life too heavy, all those who live without hope, all those who don't belie.e in a resurrection. We must carry such people to Christ to be healed.

All of us at times are carried to the Lord by the prayers of others. At Christ's feet we learn to rise and walk. There we learn that our hearts can be healed and purified. Faith means that we believe Christ can heal us. And seeing all that we have been healed of in the past, we begin already to experience the mystery of forgiveness.

There is no sin that the Lord cannot forgive. There is no illness that the Lord cannot heal. We walk toward him with timid steps, halting steps; sometimes we're carried by our brothers and sisters. Our faith begins to blossom. Then we are able, by the power of Christ in us, to say to one another, "My brother, my sister, go to Christ to have your sins forgiven. God is great and merciful and the Lover of men. Now, get up and walk. Get up. Walk. Hold your head up high and praise God."

Yes, to achieve the right dispositions for approaching Christ we should fast, we should miss some sleep, we should be mortified. But basically we should let ourselves yearn for God, as that man yearned to see Jesus. We should have faith that after we are healed we will be able to carry our brothers and sisters to Christ.

Mark 5: 1-15   *THE PRESENCE OF CHRIST*

This is a very mysterious Gospel. Those men possessed, and the swine being thrown into the sea! St. Mark places the accent on the same aspect as does St. Paul in many of his writings: on the presence of Christ. These possessed people called out, "Have you come to test us before the time?" Thus even the demons witness to Christ, the Son of God.

Mark also reports one of the rare incidences when our Lord was exposed to a reaction on the part of the pagans. They were not completely open to him and his message. In fact, they asked Christ to leave, for they were afraid of him. So he got into a boat and went into Capharnum.

In this Gospel, as in all the parables and incidents in our Lord's life, there are two aspects. One is that we understand what our Lord has done for us, as in the story of the good Samaritan, or a saying on forgiveness. The second is that we see deeply who we are and who we are meant to be to everyone we meet. We are Christ continued in space and time. We are the Church. It is the person of Jesus Christ who heals us and drives away from us those things which possess us, those things that drive us away from reality, from God.

Sometimes the presence of Christ, not only in our prayers but in events, can inspire some fear, because he is not recognized, is not familiar to us. Remember the disciples when our Lord was walking toward them in the storm, how afraid they were.

Presence is a very difficult word to talk about because there doesn't seem to be any symbol for it. Presence is the "being toward" something else, not only the "being with" or the personal awareness of another. How this presence actually exists is a matter of experience.

Christ is present to us right now. He is present here because he said he would always be with us. He is present in the very word of Scripture. Like the other modes of his presence, this presence is "toward us," so that the movement of our heart is not so much going out in search of him, or pursuing him, but simply being present to him, being "toward him," open to his presence.

We, as Christians, are called upon to meet people who are weighed down, who perhaps live in tombs in one way or another. Then this presence of ours becomes a "being for" because Christ is present in us.

In a way, there are many people who live in tombs, many people cast out of their own society, many people who are too afraid to live with other people and are afflicted. If we ourselves do not know how Christ is present to us, we can never dispel these things that drive and possess others. These forces will be driving and possessing us. Other people will not be fooled. They will see that we cannot heal, because the same diseases are in our own hearts. Our own hearts will be somewhat of a tomb where these forces live.

If you believe in your heart that Jesus is alive, that Jesus is present, if you say it with your mouth and pronounce it with your life, then Christ is present. Then much suffering and much "tomb-dwelling" can be avoided. Traditionally, in pagan times, the tombs were the dwelling places of the demons. There is a story from the fathers of the desert of one monk who of set purpose used to go and sleep on top of the tombs at night just to taunt the demons and manifest the power of Christ over them! We may not have arrived at this stage of courage, but it should inspire us with an awesome sense of the power of Christ in us to conquer all the forces within and without which seek to cut us off from the Father.

Mark 7: 31-37   *HEALING COSTS SOMETHING*

It is characteristic of St. Mark's Gospel that he takes the time and trouble to indicate some of the things that went through our Lord's heart at these periods of his life. For instance, when the leper came to him and said to him, "If you will, you can make me clean," St. Mark said our Lord was angry, not at the man, but at this instance of evil manifested in his suffering brother. He said to him, "I will, be clean."

In this Gospel, our Lord groans and looks up to heaven and then the man's ears are opened and his tongue loosened and he hears and he speaks. In all of these stories about our Lord Jesus Christ, we always learn two things: what he is now doing to and for us, and what our obligations are, what our truth-relation is to all the rest of the world, because now we are the Christ on the globe.

Our Lord is wandering outside Palestine and then he returns to the region of the "Ten Cities." Some people bring him a man and ask very pointedly that he put his hand on this person. But our Lord takes him away from the crowd and then he first opens his ears. This man then learns how to receive. Faith comes through hearing. This is a baptism story. Then the man can speak, and so Jesus is shown as the Messiah. Two or three times in the book of Isaiah this is the sign of the presence of the Messiah—that the deaf can hear, the dumb can speak, and the lame walk, and the poor hear the Gospel.

The foundation of our faith is that Jesus died and rose. Here we see Christ looking up to his Father and groaning. We know that our own healing cost him something. It cost him the passion and resurrection.

But this isn't something that happened one time and was recorded by St. Mark, and then often cited. This is the mystery that is going on all the time, because Jesus is risen and he is alive, and this presence of Christ is still opening us to receive. Then, because we are opened to receive, we are able to give, to speak, to impart Christ. Faith comes through hearing. Hearing represents any receptive act; it is not always imparted simply through talking.

Every day Christ meets us and we are still in some ways a deaf-mute. And every day we meet one another and we meet many people. Because Mark was kind enough to remember to note that Jesus groaned and looked up to heaven, maybe we can understand that healing people costs something. It takes something out of us. Sometimes it is very clear. Sometimes it is a very concrete situation. Sometimes it is a mystery of suffering that seems to have no relation at all to the Church or to any person on this globe. But if we meditate on this Gospel enough, we can understand that our own groaning, even the groaning we bring on ourselves, can open people to receive and unbind them to enable them to give.

It is not always necessary to know exactly how the healing and the opening up take place—what all the "connections" are. Why did Jesus groan? What could it possibly have cost the Son of Man to heal? Why did it take something out of him, and why at another time did he feel something go out of him when the woman with the hemorrage touched him? Because he is the Son of the living God? No. Because he is Jesus, and all the weight of being human, and all the price of imparting life was a reality that throbbed through him. Therefore it cost him something, and it will cost us something too, and for the same reason: because we bear the source of healing, which is to say, the weight of being human. Jesus died and rose. This wasn't play-acting. It is the very foundation of everything. St. Paul says, "If Jesus isn't alive, your preaching is for nothing, and your faith is a waste of time."

So we learn from this Gospel two things: what Christ has done for us, and what we are called upon to be for the world. And all this is conveyed by one word, a word we all understand very well: "Be opened." At the moment the Holy Spirit of God is here, active, moving. The Spirit of Jesus Christ is right here, talking, active. It is still Christ proclaiming his Gospel in this text. Christ is still saying to us not "Be open," as though it depended on us, but "Be open*ed*"—he does it.

The people brought the man to Jesus. He didn't come by himself. But when he was there neither did he run away. So Jesus touched him and he received, and Jesus touched him so that now he could give to others.

Can you imagine spending years in this groaning of Christ so that just once we were able to accomplish the miracle of healing somebody. It would give meaning to our whole life. Together with the Church, together in the mystery of our own individuality, we carry the weight of being human. Like Jesus we groan. Out of this groaning comes healing power. We are inserted into the mystery of Jesus' dying and rising, and this is the mystery of who we are.

Mark 8: 34-9:1   *GOD IS DEEPER THAN PAIN*

The cross is the glory of our Lord Jesus Christ. To accept that is an act of faith on our part. Jesus was tempted in everything, just as we are. Our high Priest is somebody who, because he was all beaten up, can have compassion. In other words, it was a terrible thing, humanely speaking, the cross of Jesus. The glory of that cross lies in the power of the act of love in which our Lord died, and in the light of the Spirit of holiness in which he rose. When we assert the glory of the cross of Jesus, we are asserting the greatest paradox of our own life, and we really are making an act of faith. It is faith in the fact that painfulness and humiliation involved in being human is the very sacrament by which we are united with God and can help to transform the world.

Our act of faith is that, in the act of love in which Jesus died, in that instant, all the history of the world hung in the balance. That act of dying was the most living and dynamic thing that Jesus did. Because it was such a deep and powerful act of acceptance of all that being numan means, it is of its very nature immortal. Of its nature, that act couldn't die. Resurrection is the manifestation, the overflowing into the world of space and time of the glory and power of that act in which he died. Such an act could never not be, or cease to exist. That's resurrection. And it is to that act, that act of dying and rising which was one act, that we are joined by Baptism, by faith, by the Eucharist, and by every breath we take if we want it to happen in us.

But the glory is the very thing that humiliates us and fills us with fear. Our Lord's abyss of humility was precisely that he accepted being human. He belongs to a sinful race, though sinless himself. He never denied that, and he took upon himself all the consequences of being human, death as well.

In this Gospel our Lord says, "If anyone is ashamed of me and my works. . . ." How could we be ashamed of Christ? We don't live in a culture that is overtly anti-christian. How can we deny him then? We can be ashamed of Christ if, when we suffer, we think there is something wrong. "The Gospel has failed to have an effect in my life because I am a tired, lonely human being." This is one way we can be ashamed of Christ.

"If anyone wants to come after me" presumes that our Lord is going somewhere. But there is a promise connected with the following of Christ, "Amen I say to you, that there are some of them that stand here. . . ." That promise was fulfilled in the Passion and Resurrection. That's the glory of the Son of Man. That's the promise permanently offered to us. "You are not going to die until you see the glory of the Son of Man."

Therefore, the glory of the Cross of our Lord Jesus Christ, the secret of its light, is precisely in that act of love in which we die. Every day, and at some moment in the future, that act of love in which we die is immortal and goes on forever. The resurrection of our bodies is the evidence and the manifestation in a totally human domain of the power, the life, and the beauty of that act of love in which we accept the mystery of belonging to a sinful race. And so it is a glorious thing.

Whenever we kiss the cross (actually or by accepting it in our lives) we make our act of faith and assert that the very things that fill us most with fear, the things from which we would like to run, that these are the very things which join us to our Lord and transform the world.

I really think that in life we are only free enough to face a problem when we have a dim idea that there might be a solution. Otherwise we don't face it. And for us Christians, the glory of the cross is precisely that: we can openly experience the things of which we are most afraid, which we never want to think about or face. Faith means that we believe in a solution, in the power of Christ living now, to make intercession for us, to touch us. Faith is believing that Christ pours out on us now his Spirit which enables us to live in the very same attitude in which Christ died. Through faith, the power of that reality touches us, and there is nothing we have to fear. Since we are dimly aware of a solution, we can admit to ourselves the freedom of being aware of the problem. This is the glory of the Cross: God's presence is deeper than man's problem.

Whenever we pay homage to the Cross of Christ, we are making an act of faith in the cross as a glorious reality. We acknowledge that this glory is going on right now in us. And in this act of faith, the promise of Christ is already beginning to be fulfilled in us: "You will not taste death until you see the glory of the Son of Man."

Mark 10: 46-52   *TRUTH—FORCE*

We have here the blind Bartimaeus who calls out to Jesus, the Son of David, to have mercy on him. At once he is able to see and follow Jesus. Everyone who sees this gives praise to God. Jesus went around the countryside preaching and teaching and announcing the kingdom of God by healing people of every kind of disease and infirmity.

The words of Jesus are wise words. This is not to say that they are intelligible and intellectually intelligent words! They are wise because they are powerful. The words of Jesus are what Ghandi later called "truth-force." The words of Jesus are the force of truth, a force of truth that does more than merely enlighten our minds. It heals our souls, and, if need be, it heals our bodies as well.

True wisdom is power, not subtlety. Wisdom is the very power and force of truth because truth is life. Truth is not an idea, although an idea shares in truth. An idea has light insofar as it is touched by the light of truth, but true wisdom is power. We don't come to Jesus—we are not attracted to him—in order to get another bright idea. Many people besides Christians can be more or less informed about the world, about history, even about the meaning and nature of God. Those are not the things which specify us. What specifies us is the awareness of the living relationship to Jesus Christ. If we can be enlightened by Zen-Buddhism, Hinduism, Communism, atheism, we should thank God. But what makes us Christians is the fact that the power of Jesus Christ is given to us.

When this power reaches its full light it obviously enlightens our minds also, but our minds are not the whole of reality. The words of Christ are sacramental. "Be healed" is not just a piece of information about what Jesus can do. He is not giving us another philosophy of life by his words. What is said is done.

"Blessed are the poor." What is said is done. He who admits he is poor in that very act is blessed. It is not a question of seeing how poor I can be in order to follow Christ in this new law. The Spirit of Jesus lives in us so that the words we speak, the gestures we make, the looks that we give, are meant to share in that power, and are meant to heal. Insofar as we allow ourselves to be moved by this power, we are Jesus Christ on the earth. Those who can't see and those who can't communicate can be healed by our touch.

This is the greatness of being baptized. The love in us is not a vague love for mankind in general. It is a deep personal love for every person we meet. It is a love that desires to heal the whole world, which desires the whole world to be able to see the sunshine. But this means that we have to be able to touch their eyes. When someone comes to us so bound up in prisons of fears that he can't communicate, we should be able to set him free to speak like a man, to be able to stand erect and communicate like everyone else.

We are the blind, the halt, the lame. Yes, we are the last invited to the banquet. Yes, it is to us the words are addressed, "You are blessed, poor, mourning, yearning for justice on the earth." But at the same time we are Christ. We are he who is meant to praise the Father, to offer the fruit of love that continually moves our hearts. We are meant to pray and weep and groan and strive and touch in order to bring healing to the whole world so that people can see and talk.

And, like Jesus, the words that we speak are not merely subtle and intelligent words. They only need be true words. Not the truth of a well-structured syllogism, but the truth of Jesus Christ—the wisdom and power of God.

We could feel sad that we ourselves are still so blind and unable to speak, but we also have to be joyful and proud. Even though we are not yet ourselves completely healed, we can heal, can speak, can make present on the earth the power, the "truth-force" of Jesus Christ.

Mark 15: 43-16: 8   *ANOINTING THE BODIES OF CHRIST*

The Bishops are trying to recall the nation to a respect for life. They want us to think about the gift which life is. The specific problem which is occasioning this theme is abortion, the child's right to life. Being consistent then, we ought to think of life all over the world. We have also to think of the life of two-thirds of the world today who don't have enough to eat. We have to think of the life of those who are sent over to fight and wage war. We have to think of the life of everyone in the cities who is crushed and oppressed by the pace of life, by its frantic competition, by the smog and pollution. If we're going to think of the respect for life, we have to think of all the life which God has given us which is a reflection and a sharing in the life of God. If we're going to respect life, that must include man's search for truth, his right to walk straight and up-right as a man, with the dignity of a human being. If we're going to have respect for life, then we have to be willing to die. That's what Jesus did.

But before we can die with the conviction and optimism of Jesus, we have to know, as he did, what life is all about. It would be great to live to a ripe old age and be wise and find out what life is all about, but maybe that's not what will happen to most of us. You or I could be dead this afternoon. The Lord knows that. But if we're willing to know what life is all about and to share that life with others, then our life would make sense—and our death too, whenever that happens.

These myrrh-bearing women who brought ointments for the body of Jesus in this Gospel were doing all that they could to respect life. They had gone to anoint what they thought would be the dead body of Jesus. Everyone else had given up trying to do anything. The disciples, the future pillars of the Church, were all someplace else. The crowd had gone home. Pilate was probably still in bed, and Herod too (definitely Herod!). But these three women did the obvious. They did the only thing left to do: anoint the body of Jesus. And they were the ones who heard the beautiful words, "You're looking for Jesus who was crucified. He is risen. He is not here."

How can we ever feel helpless when the Gospel tells us that the first experience of the Resurrection was given to people who were doing the only thing left to do: show respect for life?

What is life? Life is something so great that even the tomb can't snuff it out. That's the whole point of the story. Everything that is somehow shares in this mystery of life. Everything that is, is alive with the life of God. The tragedy is that we live in a world of violence. It confuses us and we don't know how to respect life in a world of violence. Only in Jesus can we see the wisdom which consists in being able to touch and appreciate life even in the midst of violence. By allowing the *responsibility* for that violence to touch us, we can, in Christ, transform it into life.

In a way, Jesus was violent. He was eaten up with the love of his Father. He had, you might say, the violence of the peaceful. He so loved peace that he allowed violence to have its way with him. For the love of his Father he respected all life. Like Christ, we too must be extremely gentle in order to protect life, but gentle with a ferocity for peace.

Life and the passing on of life means maturity. It means the maturity of the full age of Jesus Christ. We can't afford the luxury of feeling hopeless. Even if all we can do is find the dead body of Jesus and anoint it, let's go and do that. In that act of reverence we will hear that he is alive. Yes, he is being crucified all over the world, in alcoholics, in dope addicts, in prisoners. If we think that these are all dead bodies and without hope, let's go and anoint them anyway. In the depth of every person there is the seed of life. Let us at least be strong enough for that anointing. Then we too will be amazed to hear that death and violence have not conquered at all. Everyone is risen!

Luke 2: 41-52   *MARY LOOKS FOR GOD*

As Luke recounts this story in the Gospel, he means us to see in it one more step in the revelation of who

Christ is. The incidents in the infancy Gospel are often modeled on Old Testament passages, especially those recounting the infancy of the prophet Samuel.

It is as though Luke were saying that all that the prophets did and said find their distillation in the reality of Christ. In him all the lines of the Old Testament revelation finally converge in one fine point of radiant light. Our text is full of mystery. Why did our Lord give such an answer to our Lady and to St. Joseph? Why was there in the temple such questioning and the answering of questions? Why, at the age of twelve, did he make this revelation of himself and assert his heavenly origin, over against the anxious worry of our Lady and St. Joseph?

We could take any one of these questions or all of them and tracing back their allusions to Old Testament themes, weave a rich tapestry of revelation concerning our Lord Jesus.

I am more struck by our Lady's attitude than by anything else. Did it ever occur to you that even our Lady had to look for God? She lost him, and had to look for him. The center of the Holy Family was Christ, but in this incident we see Mary who was just praised in this same Gospel for her great faith, now searching for God. Why didn't she just say to herself, "Well, God is the Prime Mover. Nothing whatever happens without his divine will. I think I'll just go home." It would have been a very "reasonable" approach, but Christianity is too deep for that. Faith does not absolve us from experiencing human life. Rather, it frees us to experience it in all its depths.

Mary is the Mother of God, but she is also the mother of this lost boy, and she is responsible for him, loves him, and so she looks after him. The Mother of God was not insulated from being a human being. She lived by faith and that is why she was not scared of being scared. She lived out her human reality.

Now St. Luke, who has just presented us with the virgin birth, puts on our Lady's lips the words, "Your father and I have sought you sorrowing." As though this losing of Christ had welded our Lady and St. Joseph more closely together than anything in their previous experience. It is as though the searching for Christ is what made a family, a community, out of their relationship.

So they find Christ. We who are accustomed to romantic movies expect some sort of happy ending. But our Lord replies, "Why did you look for me? Did you not know that I must be in my father's house?" And Mary kept all these things in her heart, pondering over them. And, after such an independent reply, the child went down with them and was obedient to them.

Mary is the exemplar of the Church. This means, in this case, that the Church will have to go around and look for Christ. But the mystery is that we cannot really look unless somehow we know God. Otherwise it is not a search but a panic. Then you are not looking for Christ, but, like losing a security blanket, are seeking him because you need something to make you happy. We must search for Christ because we love him, because the loss of him brings out a deeper love of him than we ever suspected that we had. If we search for Christ together, we become a community. If we look to one another to supply for the absence of Christ, we can become a bunch of frustrated misfits.

Saint-Exupery once said, "Love is not so much looking at one another, as everyone looking together in the same direction." Such looking does not preclude awareness of one another; rather it heightens it. But a community is not a juxtaposed group of individuals each searching for Christ. It is a deep union between people who are searching together for Christ: the Christ that faith makes them dimly remember, and the Christ who sustains them in each other as they search.

Let us pray to the Holy Mother of God that we may share her faith and know the mystery of the searching for Christ. Sometimes, even in sorrow, let us search with that delicate awareness of the other, which makes the finding of Christ a mutual and ever-deeper joy.

Luke 4: 16-30   *JUST AN ORDINARY GUY*

From the Gospel we learn that Our Lord was a scandal. They found him too much to accept. They were scandalized in him. The scandal came because Our Lord was of such lowly origin. They knew his father, or at least the man they thought was his father. They knew his mother, his cousins: brothers and sisters. They were all around. This is the reason why God wasn't accepted, and this incident in the Gospel is a kind of distillation of that familiar stumbling block: he was too familiar. Everybody knew him.

It is interesting, you know, when you think of it, that God—Christ—could have dazzled us with his power if he had wanted to. He could have done it that way. Had Our Lord wanted to impress us with the greatness of his coming, he could have struck us with fear. But one of the reasons why Our Lord was not accepted in his own home town was perhaps because he was too familiar, and that familiarity came from the fact that everybody knew Joseph who was the local carpenter.

This Joseph is now the patron of the whole Church. This man was presumed by Christians to have been holy since he was the lawful spouse of the Virgin Mary through marriage, and was the guardian of Christ. This man was presumed to have been holy, but not much more thought was ever given to him.

His career now is the same as when he was on earth. For centuries the Church never really gave him much thought. When she did, she realized that his greatness was such that of all the saints of the Church:the Popes, the Bishops, priests and missionaries, holy women of all ages, he is the one most apt to be the patron of the Church.

If we follow on the road that made St. Joseph the patron of the Church, our great challenge will be not to lose courage in following him. Are other people going to be scandalized? Sure! We're all going to be scandalized. The world we're always talking about still dwells to some degree in us. The reason which made St. Joseph so great—this man who perhaps could have done many other things besides spending his life in a small town—is that he believed that the woman he married and the son he didn't father were respectively the Mother and the Son of God. This man who lived in this small town, in faith, did what everyone else was doing, but did it more profoundly, cooperating with God. This man must have been a scandal once in a while even to himself! We know he was a stumbling block to his neighbors' acceptance of Christ because there was nothing great about him.

Men are troubled today with this power of being able to control the material universe. For centuries we stood outside these efforts and looked at it and said that it was not good. A man like Joseph would not have been accused of that. He had to earn his living. He had to work to eat. And don't you think that the depth of his sympathy and understanding of his fellow men lies in the fact that he himself had to live and work and stay in Nazareth?

Now we understand that the aspirations of man to fashion the material universe are noble in themselves and are really an extension of the redemption to heal suffering, to do away with poverty. These things are or seem to be noble and fundamentally from the Spirit of God. But our duty is not foolishly to jump on somebody's band wagon, but rather to think out our own Christian vocation in the light of someone like Joseph. We are going to find that we are forced to bring all these aspirations into the mystery of the Incarnation, and that is going to look so ordinary because it is so authentic. And that is going to be a stumbling block! Our greatest danger is that we will accept somebody else's values and not Christ's. We won't want to be a stumbling block. But it is only the life of faith which is going to keep us centered on the one point of light—Christ.

Men look at the world and at the average human existence and say it is a scandal. They call it absurd, unintelligible. They call it the meaninglessness of existence, but this is the very thing we are called to live. To really live love as it is every day, not using Christianity as an insulation against being worried and tired and misunderstood. To do this, day after, day, for the love of Christ and the love of his brethren, is to provide the depths of our soul with an authenticity and a peace that can never be taken away. Our danger is not so much that we won't continue in this way, as that we will allow ourselves to be influenced by other judgments. We won't do anything. We won't grow very much, and instead of being like St.Joseph, a radiant witness to a meaningful existence, we will become just second-rate organizers of this world. Religion then will cramp us and instead of being able to dedicate ourselves to material progress, we will have to compromise with it in order to save our religion.

The other way is to follow with such a depth of conviction that we stop short of nothing but this simple, ordinary, imminent activity in which the world really sees what Christ has done to human existence: sanctified every bit of it.

So we should pray for all the world. Man's highest vocation according to one half of the world is to work, but the drive behind that work is resentment, because this world does not yield a sufficient security. We should pray for these people, and for ourselves too, so that we really live by faith, and find the greatest authentic witness to the reality of the Gospel in being able to see the depths of our life now—always a scandal to a part of us and to part of the world, but ultimately the thing for which the human soul is really yearning.

Luke 5: 1-11   *BUT WE'VE ALREADY TRIED!*

This Gospel is St. Luke's own version of the vocation of the disciples. It is typical of him to place this in the context of the power of the Word of God. The crowd was by the side of the seashore, anxious to hear the Word of God explicitly. St. Mark explains that he was so crowded that he asked for a boat so that he could see everyone and they him. When he had finished giving the Word of God to the people he turned to Simon and addressed the Word to him: "Go out into the deep water and lower your nets." Simon's reply was a tentative act of faith: "We were hard at work all night and caught nothing at all; but if you say so, I will let down the nets." So he went and did so.

The Word of God spoken in Christ and through Christ is creative. And so at the word of Christ the nets were filled. The boats were filled to near overflowing; Peter, as it were, had in his boat, in the catch of fish, the concrete response and effect of Christ's Word. That kind of effectiveness brings upon us a sense of our unworthiness: "Get away from me, Lord, don't come near me. I am a sinful man." But again he hears the Word of God: "Don't be afraid. From now on not only will you be forgiven, not only will you be joined to my company, but you will be a fisher of men. Yes, you Peter, miserable little fisherman, sinner, will be the person who brings others into the kingdom of God." That is the last word of this incident.

And so they put their boats on the shore and their response to Jesus' invitation is one of real faith: they drop everything, leave everything, and follow him. Luke's view of all this allows us to see that this call is not only about the disciples' lifetime response to Jesus; it is God's Word daily addressed to each one of us.

Peter might have said: "I have been fishing for 35 years. I know it isn't a good time for fishing. Besides, I've been out all night. I know how good it is—it isn't good at all!" Luke simply gives as Peter's response, "At your word, I'll lower the nets."

This frequently happens in our own lives. We are confronted with something which is undoubtedly the Word of God for us, but it doesn't look too sensible, too smart. But something inside us says to go out anyway and lower the nets and see what happens. Often in such circumstances we are less articulate or acquiescent than Peter. We *know* it is stupid.

We know because we've tried it before and it just doesn't work. "Things and people don't change." "You can't change human nature!" "That's life!" And on and on with all the clichés we can think of. But sometimes above and beyond all these rationalizations there is the vague sense that if we don't gamble now, something way down deep will be perverted. So off we go!

Perhaps each of us has seen a catch of fish, despite all the odds against it. When it happens, our first response is like Peter's: we are aware of being a sinner—which is wonderful because it's true. Awareness of our sinfulness makes us want to get out of God's presence—"Get away, Lord, I am a sinful man."

Sometimes we actually run away. This is a very imperfect response. The one thing that it has in its favor is that it's authentic—it comes from our hearts.

So too with Peter; his was an authentic response. St. Luke does not record any great moral improvement as Peter made his way back to the shore. And yet this is the man who is made the fisher of men. Why? Perhaps because he was the best example of how the Word of God works in us: hesitant faith, reluctant action, sense of unworthiness, fears calmed by Christ.

Luke 8: 3-15 *LETTING THE SEED GROW*

This Gospel is a Gospel of life. The mystery of our own lives is scattered in great prodigality all over the earth by God. As our Lord first preached this Gospel he was reflecting his own experience as a preacher. He scattered the seed of the Word everywhere he went. As he looked behind him he could see that some never bore any fruit; some simply disappeared altogether; some began to grow but was choked; some really grew to fruition. And so he took the image from his own experience and he said, "The kingdom of God is like a sower who went out into his field to sow seed." The disciples ask him what it means, and disciples ever after have been asking the same question. Later on, in their own lives of preaching, they would also experience what Jesus experienced about the Word.

In the Mass we say, "Blessed are you, Lord of all creation. Through your goodness we have this bread to offer, which the earth has given and human hands have made. It will become for us the bread of life." "Blessed are you, God of all creation. Through your goodness you have scattered your seed of the Word over all the earth. We gather the life produced by this seed and we offer it to you that it may become more alive with the great power of your own life."

The seed is planted in our hearts. At times it lies open, or is stepped on, or is choked. Sometimes it grows. Insofar as it produces and bears fruit in us, the whole mystery of life is present in us. It is this seed which is transforming us day after day.

Faith means that we cherish this seed. Faith means that we let this seed grow. Faith means that we don't let it get choked by the cares and worries and fears and pains and failures of life. What will the seed grow to be? What will the fruit look like? What kind of flower will it be? It will be God's deepest ideas and ambitions for me and for you and for all of us together. We will be gathered from the four corners of the earth and blended into one living bread, one living flower, which will be the body and the beauty of Christ.

We know, maybe in a vague sort of way at times, but we know generally what things block our true life from flowering. We may not know exactly where we're going, but that's because we don't know exactly who we are. We do know that we are called to live the life of God. God's life is a movement of love. We are meant to reflect this love. So the seed of love falls on our earth (for we are earth), and it begins to grow. The wind, the dew, the sun, the rain, the warmth of the breath of God brings the seed to life and gradually changes us into himself.

If we can go beyond our failures, beyond our own thinking, and cling to this seed of love, it will infallibly grow, it will produce fruit. The fruit will be a hymn of love, a beautiful flower. And we, who cannot make the seed come or grow, can *allow it to grow.* As it grows we come to know who we are.

We often wish we were "unearthly." If our lives were not really of this earth, there would be nothing to transform. If our lives did not share the pain and failure and darkness of life, then we could not be the soil for the Word. The Word would not have flesh out of which it could transform itself and live and be of this earth.

The seed that is planted in us takes a lifetime to come to full fruition. If, beyond all our ideas, beyond all our efforts, beyond all success or failure, we cling to the life deep within our being, then out of our tears and out of the earth which we are will come the fragrance of God's love, a perfume that will fill the whole world. The good heart that produces the seed of the Word and allows it to come to full flower is the human being who has given himself over completely to the growing, life-giving action of God. The very earth which produced our bodies is then transformed by the true seed of the Word and returns again to God in a rhythm of praise.

Luke 8: 40-48   *PLEASE TOUCH*

All three synoptic Gospels carry an account of this healing by Christ. All three follow the same order. Our Lord is on his way to heal the daughter of the ruler of the synagogue when his journey is interrupted by a woman of faith; then he proceeds on his way to heal the daughter. The reason for writing the story that way, as the early Fathers saw it, was to offer readers an understanding of the mystery of the church of the Gentiles: the Messiah on the way to heal the "synagogue" (the Jewish people) is touched by the faith of the Gentile church and power goes out of him to heal it.

People, then, are healed by touching Christ. How do we touch Christ today? How can we, with the crowd all around Jesus, first recognize him, then work our way close to him, then reach out and touch the tassle of his cloak? The answer is faith, not a faith in Jesus as some abstraction, but as a living reality. Jesus does not heal us as an idea or a theory, but as a gentle, firm, powerful, compassionate person.

I wonder if perhaps we couldn't ask ourselves whether we really look hard enough for Jesus, whether or not in the crowd of our own activities and emotions, hustle and bustle, we search out the person of Jesus and reach out and touch him. Again, not reaching out to some cosmic force or ethereal help, but to Jesus himself. I wonder if we pray enough; I don't mean precisely if we spend enough *time* in prayer, though that is part of it. I mean, is there *depth* in our prayer, so that when we pray we are actually reaching out to touch Jesus.

There is another aspect to these incidents in the Gospel story. Our Lord teaches by actions as well as by words. He is teaching us in this incident not to be afraid to reach out toward him with the arms of faith.

In the Gospels, especially St. Luke's, the power to heal, which is identified with the Holy Spirit, is always connected with prayer. St. Luke tells us, for instance, that our Lord went away in prayer to God, and then he chose the twelve apostles. These apostles then became also messengers of healing. As Jesus walks about, power goes forth from him to heal. Jesus goes about healing and doing good. "The Spirit of God is upon me to preach the Gospel to the poor, give sight to the blind, heal the lame and the deaf."

One of the deepest desires in our souls today, one which is in evidence all over the world in many men who have hardly heard at all about Christ, is the desire to heal. It is a desire to heal the wounds in men's bodies from bullets, from the A bomb, from policemen's clubs. It is a desire to wipe away the tears that come from tear gas and loneliness, from the differences between the "have" and the "have nots," the North and South Vietnamese, the whites and the blacks, white Canadians and Indians, Germany and Russia, France and England. Humanity lies ripped open, and every human heart bleeds, suffering from an issue of blood. If we pray with faith, if, despite the crowd and human respect, despite the loneliness, despite the confusion, despite our doubts as to whether or not we'll ever be able to touch his garment—if despite all these things we reach out and touch Jesus, then the Spirit of God will rest on us.

But not only that. We too are meant to be Christ for one another. If we touch Christ and his power enters into us, then someone can touch us and power will go forth from us too and people will be healed. This must be so, else how can the mystery of Christ's presence to man, God's revelation of love, continue?

The power that came forth from Jesus was due to his complete openness to the Spirit of the Father. Let us ask ourselves if we really pray in faith. Are we healed enough ourselves so that others can reach out and touch us and be healed?

Luke 10: 23-37   *SHIFTING THE CENTER OF GRAVITY*

St. Paul tells us that it is through Christ that we have such great confidence in our relationship with God; it is not that we are self-sufficient and can take personal credit for anything, but our sufficiency is from God.

A certain theologian stood up one day and asked Jesus (this itinerant preacher, this layman), "Master, what must I do to inherit eternal life?" And Jesus, speaking the language of the theologian, asked him, "What is the theological tradition on this? How does it read in the Law?" And the theologian replied, basing himself on the best rabbinic tradition, combining Deut 6:5 and Lev 19:18, "Love the Lord your God with your whole heart, and with your whole soul and with all your strength, and with all your mind; and your neighbor as yourself." Our Lord said, "That is the right answer. Do that, and you shall live."

And the man said, "Who is my neighbor?" "How far do I extend this thing?" Notice the question, because as our Lord answers him we are going to see the dimension of the New Law, the law that we don't take for ourselves, create for ourselves, but the law that is given to us.

And so our Lord tells the story of the man who goes down from Jerusalem to Jericho, who was beaten and left half dead. As a good semitic storyteller, our Lord has three people go by. First, a priest, then the Levite; now everyone is expecting a conclusion, a turning point in the story.

And our Lord said, "This North Vietnamese soldier—or Russian soldier in Czechoslovakia, or this Negro in the slums, or this fellow hung up on drugs—comes along." That is the way the word "Samaritan" sounded to Jewish ears. Notice that the inquirer, in answering, cannot even say the "Samaritan," but rather "the one who had compassion or treated him with pity!"

The man our Lord now picks as the example of fulfillment of the Law is, in the mind of this lawyer, this theologian, this expert among the Hebrew people, the very antithesis of anyone who could be keeping the Law. This Samaritan, moved with compassion, treats the injured man on the road, carries him to an inn, and pays for his keep.

And then our Lord asks a question: "Now who do you think was neighbor to the man who was left on the road?" Do you see how the center of gravity shifts? The man asks, "Who is my neighbor, how far do I push this love thing?" and our Lord answers, "Who was neighbor to this man?"

If we ask the question, "Who is *my* neighbor?" the center of gravity is myself. The whole center of my consideration is me, and how far do *I* go in this loving business, and how virtuous am *I*, and how Christian am *I*, and can *I* love everybody? I, I, I. But as our Lord rephrases the question, the center of the gravity is the other person. The point of the revelation is, "Who was neighbor to the man who was wounded?" not "Was the wounded man a neighbor to the Samaritan?" or "Did the Samaritan push the law of love far enough?"

The early Fathers used to love to make our Lord this Samaritan. Do you think God kept the Law? Do you think God loved his neighbor as himself? Suppose God had asked that question: "Who is my neighbor?" Anyone want to stand up and say, "I am God's neighbor?" But suppose you put it the other way: "Was God a neighbor to us?" Neighbor means comrade, friend, companion. Who was the friend? God was a friend to us, God was neighbor to us because he made us the center of attraction, the center of his consideration; but no one is neighbor to God. How could God say, "How far should I push this thing?" If we love the way our Lord does, then the center of gravity is every person we meet, and we are neighbor to him because he is the center of importance, not ourselves.

Sometimes, even when we talk about love, unconsciously we are so self-centered that the question is: "Have *I* loved, or failed to love, or have *I* pushed this thing far enough, or was *I* just or not loving to my neighbor?" But look at the way the Son of God acted toward us. The center of gravity, of attention, for him was not how much he should love the human race, but the other way around: "The human race, my brothers, mankind is in need and I am moved to pity and therefore, automatically I am neighbor to them."

Now this law is written in our hearts. This is a gift. I don't know whether any human being could ever be that selfless if left to himself. But we are not supposed to be self-sufficient; our self-sufficiency is not from us. "It was through Christ that we have confidence in God."

It is through Christ that we know God has proved himself neighbor to us. If in the power of his Spirit, and in great freedom, the other person becomes the center of attraction, the center of interest, then, though we may stand on one spot on this globe and never move, we are neighbor to every person in the whole human race. Then our prayer and our compassion: these gifts of the Spirit of God, can reach out and pour wine and oil on the wounds of mankind.

It may even be that this shift in the center of our gravity comes about precisely when we stop trying to provide for ourselves and realize how much God loves us, that God has proved himself neighbor to us. We don't have to provide for ourselves. We can step into reality and let the "other" be the center of our attraction. And then, in a way, we can prove ourselves neighbor to God because then God is the center of our attention.

This Samaritan, this down-and-outer, this heretic, is the example our Lord gives us of someone who fulfills this law: love of God and love of neighbor, and he does it with an utterly simple concern for someone else. Notice in the story, our Lord never mentions that the Samaritan thinks of the Law or even of God: he saw someone in need and he went to him. This man proved himself a neighbor. To live like that is always a new creation; it is the work of the Spirit of God. So let us pray for one another that we can get out of the boundaries we have established for our own self-preservation and be neighbor to everyone on this globe. And let us thank God that we do have "neighbor relations" with God through Christ.

Luke 10: 38-42   *GOD AND MAN ARE NOT RIVALS*

The deepest thing we are called upon to do is to cling to God and to search for God and never, never stop looking for God. The very fact that we search for God opens us up every day to be rid of our illusions. Everyday, what we thought was a search for God turns out to be an illusion, and we have to start again. Yet the moment we stop searching for God we lose him.

This may sound a bit extreme but we have to be extreme because God is extreme. God is extremely beyond us; God is extremely deep in us; God is extremely powerful; God is extremely tender.

Everyday we make an idol, and every day by the mercy of God that idol is smashed and we start again. Why do we look for God like that? Because God in us is looking for himself. God in us is going back to himself. There is only one thing necessary because there is only one God. Beyond all our illusions and all our searching and all our little gods, there is God.

The deepest wound in our soul is the conviction that God and man are rivals. We think that when we exalt God we lessen man, and when we exalt man we make God less. So it often seems to us that we have to make a choice, do one or the other. Too often we say: "God is so severe. God is so far away. I think I will make a little god of my own, a little closer, not quite so extreme, not quite so far away, not quite so hard to figure out. God Himself is so hard to figure out, so unable to be manipulated. I can't manipulate the true God, so I think I'll make a little god of my own."

God rivals only one thing: a human being turned in upon himself. To such a person God surely is a rival, because God is God. God creates, God redeems, God cares, God comes, God abides, and God binds up wounds. And men? I turn in upon myself, and do I find infinite life? No. I find chaos, and I cling to that. I don't create, redeem, heal, serve, move to help. God is my rival in these things.

God and man are not rivals. God made man, God heals man, God loves man. The idolatry of turning in on ourselves is what creates a multitude of idols that bewitch us, seduce us, that makes us afraid. The gods of security and comfort, the gods of knowledge and status, the gods of power and being right—we are so afraid to offend these gods that we worship them. But God, the true God, lies out beyond our idolatry, lies deep within our very depths.

Let us cling to the true God. Let us not be afraid of offending the false ones, of incurring their displeasure. Let us not worship "just in case" – just in case there really is a true God and we have made sure we gave attention to all gods. Let us worship the one true God and Jesus Christ whom he has sent.

And as we get used to the desert of not having gods around to console us and build us up and give us security, our whole human nature cries out. And in this crying out God is already present, sustaining us. Our weakness somehow becomes the strength of God. We are protected now from the assaults of evil and malice and idolatry. God simply must come to our rescue. We are now so weak that God must come to be our life. In the very depth of this emptiness God comes to heal and purify and strengthen and guide and console. Then God reveals to us that he is not our rival but our friend.

Luke 11: 14-27   *NOTHING REAL WITHOUT JOY*

When we meditate on the Gospels we have to ask ourselves two questions: What did Our Lord mean when he first said these things; secondly, what does the Church see and understand by these words? In all the things Christ did and said, why are only such and such particular events recorded and not others?

We are always meant to look back at the life of Christ through the event of the Resurrection. The Church drew from this story not fear but consolation. Our Lord says, "I have overcome temptation." The power of Christ is sufficient to cast out evil. This power, this finger of God (St. Matthew calls it the Spirit of God), this power of Christ is his work in us.

We can see ourselves as we read this text. Many times in the Gospel the man who is cured by Christ is blind or dumb. At the touch of Christ he can speak of what he sees. He is going to proclaim the Good News, the fact of his own healing by Jesus Christ.

This provokes a great division in the people. Some say, "This man has a devil." Others say, "Show us a sign." And Our Lord, as is typical of all his answers, appeals to nothing but the intrinsic reality of what has happened. Nothing can refute this argument. It is in that light that he applies a norm not only valid for the kingdom of Satan but for the kingdom of God as well: "A kingdom divided against itself cannot stand. . .he who is not with me is against me."

This Gospel is supposed to be a meditation on the power of Christ, which ought to give rise to certainty, to confidence. We're supposed to "fear not" because Christ has overcome the world. None of us need wonder if there are evil drives in us or whether there are forces in us strong enough to impel us to evil. Unless we admit these realities we are not hearing the Word aright.

But the great norm of judgment in Christianity is the result which the Word produces in us. Nothing in Christianity is real until it gives rise to peace, joy, and confidence. No experience is fully Christian until it is a source of peace. Otherwise, the depth of the message would be foolish: "If Christ be not risen, then your faith is vain." It is a waste of time.

It is quite possible that as we grow in appreciation of the reality of our lives and existence, we can temporarily be overcome by the tragic sense of evil, opposition, weakness and failure. This is good because it is true. Yet we know that in faith we haven't seen the reality until joy, peace, and confidence are present. But this is why the Gospels were written: so that our experience might make sense to us in faith when we are overwhelmed: he will be there. When the boat going across the water is just about to sink, the disciples say to Our Lord, "Master, does it mean nothing to you that we are going under?" If at that point we are still clinging to faith, we are going to know the reality of Christ standing up and calming the waves. This is simply another manifestation of the primordial power which orders the chaos.

Every experience in life, including death, makes us rise in the glory of the risen Christ. This Gospel is meant to tell us that Christ has power over everything we experience. We accept it and embrace it in faith, and this Word of God in our hearts, embraced in faith under the power of the Spirit, is nurtured, developed, and becomes a great tree, a lily, or a rose, and grows into something beautiful. Its soil is the great experience of life and living.

Because our experience is not real as a Christian experience until we know the power and joy that comes from knowing Christ, the Gospel ends with the response to the woman in the crowd: "Happy are they who hear the Word of God and keep it." They hear it and give it existence. And unless a Christian experience gives rise to a deeper sense of the presence of Christ, it isn't complete. Our effort is not to escape but to allow life to have an effect in us which can only be a deeper sense of joy and confidence and compassion.

Luke 14: 15-24   *CHILDREN OF MERCY*

This is a beautiful Gospel. It contains one of the parables our Lord Jesus gave us so that we might hold in our hearts in a special way the mystery of God's mercy.

The only thing that disqualifies from the kingdom is lack of interest. Those whom the Master decreed would never taste of his supper were those who refused to come. Those who were actually at the banquet were the poor, the blind, the halt, and the lame. They were the people who were forced to come in, who were led by the hand to the banquet because, with typical oriental deference, they refused to enter the house of a great man. But the Master, intent that his house be full, sent his servants to force them, to coax them, to urge them to enter.

In the prophecy of Ezekiel we hear the Lord God promise us that with the gift of his Spirit we would have a heart—not of stone—but of flesh. What changes the heart of someone? What softens hearts? The gift of love. And the Lord God has given us that gift. We are the poor, the blind, the halt, and the lame. We are those who were wandering about the highways and byways of the world. We are the ones who were forced to come into the banquet. That is who we really are.

In an effort nowadays to achieve "self-identity" we sometimes skip the first step of self-recognition: that we are the objects of unmerited mercy. When St. John asks, "How can the love of God exist in a man who sees his brother in need and closes his heart to him?" he is not telling us that social service is the essence of Christianity. He is simply reminding us that when the Lord saw us in need He did not close his heart to us; this is how we know what love is. He laid down his life for us because he saw us in need.

There are so many paradoxes in Christianity. The completeness of our dedication to Jesus, the irrevocability of our baptism and the totality of the death to self to which we are called; and on the other hand the simplicity, the joy and the childlikeness in which all these great and awesome realities are supposed to transpire. What holds these seemingly diverse realities together? The answer is the mercy of God as it exists in our hearts, a deep, personal awareness of the mercy in which we are invited to the banquet. The greatest tragedy in life would be to forget about the mercy of God. Because then, not only would our heart once again become hard and closed to our brother in need, but we would lose the freedom of access to Christ himself for our lives would no longer be based on who we really are.

The freedom to which we are called, the joy which is a gift to us, is precisely the unmerited mercy of the Lord by which we are present at his banquet. This is not an abstraction. Who of us could say that we are worthy of sharing in the Eucharist? No one. From the highways and byways, from the "labyrinthian ways of our own minds" and hearts we have been brought to the banquet hall of the Lord. We have been brought by the grace of God.

Of all the people who have ever lived, are living now, or who will follow us, how many have known about Christ? How many who have know him have loved him! And of those who have loved, how many have returned so much as a fraction of what he has done for us? Whatever love of Christ is in our hearts, it is a great act of God's mercy. To be in love with Christ is to be in the banquet hall. We should always have this humble awareness that we were forced to come. Let the pain of this realization be your greatest treasure, and let the joy of it praise God. Then your heart will never be closed to your brother, because you will know that the Lord has never closed his heart to you. Then the praise of God: the Father, Son, and Holy Spirit will rise from your heart.

Luke 16: 1-13   *NO TIME TO LOSE*

This short and in some ways very mysterious parable is a lasting witness to the profundity and the fruitfulness of our Lord's words. The parable itself probably continues down as far as the words which the steward addressed to the man who owed 100 bushels of wheat. Then comes the statement of St. Luke, that the Lord (meaning there our Lord, not the lord in the parable) praised this dishonest steward for his astuteness and for being enterprising.

There then follows three other statements of our Lord, probably uttered at different times and added here so that the early Christian preacher could develop the parable in any one of three directions. The first is the statement that the children of this world are more astute in dealing with their own kind than are the children of light. The second is our Lord's saying about the use of the money, followed by the saying about those who are entrusted with little things and, being found capable, are entrusted with greater things. And then the last saying, that no servant can be the slave of two masters. All three sayings betray a play on words in the original Aramaic.

The early Christian preacher, basing himself on any

one of these three latter statements of our Lord, could develop his commentary on the parable and still never exhaust its profundity. We have all heard many dissertations on these three themes but perhaps we haven't considered sufficiently the main theme, the one presented by our Lord in the parable itself.

The main theme is not concerned with the misuse of money nor how enterprising we should be in the use of the goods of this world. It is a call to the children of God to be watchful and enterprising and completely dedicated in their response to the fact of the Risen Christ. When our Lord taught this parable he tried to tell the men who were there right in front of him that the time was *now*, that the kingdom of God was breaking in and there was no time to be lost in preparing for it. Just as the steward found himself with no time to lose and had to use all his wits to save himself, so anyone confronted with the Gospel message cannot afford to dilly-dally around, but must make a decision; having once made that decision, he must continue to live its implications all of his life.

I remember watching the Crucifixion scene of "Ben Hur" being filmed in Rome. That same one-minute scene was done nine times over in one afternoon, and it may be that none of the scenes shot that day ever got into the movie. The children of this world surely are enterprising!

How many times on TV we see some great artist: a ballet dancer, a pianist, a conductor, perform for hours in complete absorption, utterly dedicated to his art. Or just consider the all-absorbing preoccupation of a great corporation president. Indeed, the children of this world are enterprising.

Nor can we hide our own sloth by saying that such things don't interest us. The man engaged in such enterprises may ask us, "Well, what does interest you?" If we reply, "Jesus Christ," then he can say to us, "Do you really believe that Jesus Christ is in every man, woman, and child? Do you believe that the Christ is risen and alive, and that he is to be loved and served in himself and in every one you meet?" And if we reply "Yes" then he has every right to say to us, "Then why aren't you as enterprising in this affair as I am in mine?"

The Church preserved this parable, out of the many that our Lord uttered, because it is a call to us now, telling us that we have no time to waste. We must take a stand and make a decision. The Church itself, by its reality, is meant to be a living parable, called upon to make just such a decision. At the same time, you and I are called to hear the words of this Gospel and realize that we too must be enterprising as we are confronted with this eternal message of Christ.

The heart of our Lord's words, the idea behind all his parables is this: "You heard it, now take a stand. Make it deeper. Make it more real. You believe that the kingdom of God is everything. Now say it over and over again, deeper every time. Because if you do, you will possess the joy of this kingdom, and through you the world will be able to know Jesus Christ. The world will be presented with the fact of Christ and receive the privilege of making a decision."

We have no other certainty and security than Jesus. We are the salt of the earth. If we do not present Christ to the world, then we are fit to be thrown out and trampled upon. But for us this means a decision. Putting all our eggs in one basket, not saving one or two just in case Jesus is not enough.

Let us then before the sun goes down today, ratify this message of Christ addressed to us, take it into our hearts more deeply, and by that very fact become the sacrament to the world, presenting man with the true face of Christ. The kingdom of God is still breaking in upon us.

Every moment is a moment of decision. The grace that we have is the grace of knowing the joy of the Good News, and accepting the responsibility of having heard the message and therefore knowing the freedom, the joy, of life in the risen Christ.

Luke 18: 9-14   *GOD IS A PUSHOVER*

I suppose in some ways we have become so used to the paradox implied in this parable that when we hear it we are tempted to relax and say, "We've heard all that before."

The prayer of the Pharisee was a very common prayer in his day. The rabbinical writings contain prayers that are similar to this one. They often begin, "My God, I thank you. . . ." Our Lord may be giving comments on such prayers in this parable, the least untouched of the parables that have come down to us.

The things that this man speaks of doing imply not merely keeping the law. They are over and above it. The law calls for fasting once a year. The Pharisee in this story fasts twice a week. He gives tithes of all he possesses. What this man is speaking to God about is his capacity to go over and beyond the law.

The tax-gatherer, on the other hand, was the most despised man in his culture, a kind of quisling. He was taken from among the people by the Roman government, and it was up to him to impose land taxes and collect them for the government. He made most of his money by accepting bribes and not giving the full assessment of the land, thereby saving the man some taxes. He was mistrusted by the Roman system, and despised by his own people. He was a crook, and this was the way he made his money.

Now when this man went to the temple, he didn't have a ghost of a chance to change his life. What would he do if he stopped being a tax collector? He could get no other job with the Romans. His own people didn't speak to him. In other words, this man backed himself in such a corner by his crooked deals that no human being could or would have anything to do with him.

And so the comparison is not between a proud man and a humble sinner, but between a zealous Pharisee and a crooked dealer who had backed himself into such a corner that he was beyond human help.

St. Luke sets this parable in a context of prayer. The story just before it is about the importunate widow and the unjust judge. This parable belongs in the context of prayer. The prayer of the heart, the Jesus Prayer, is often called in tradition the "prayer of the tax gatherer" or the "prayer of the Publican."

The paradox in what our Lord said doesn't come in the description of these two men so much, because he could be describing a life situation: the suffering, the loneliness, the despised nature of this tax collector. Where else could he go for relief but to God? The paradox comes in the next line: "I tell you, this tax gatherer went home justified and not the other, for everyone who exalts himself shall be humbled, and whoever humbles himself will be exalted."

The simple, painful recognition of the truth before God and a plea for mercy is sufficient to justify a man before God, while a constant, reiterated practice of what passes for virtue does not justify a man.

I wonder if that is really the God *we* pray to? Do we know that no matter what kind of bind we can get ourselves into, through our own stupidity and sinfulness, that it is enough to beat our breasts and say, "God, be merciful to me a sinner?" The man our Lord describes didn't get out of his bind. His life situation didn't change. But he was changed in his depths because God had come to him.

This parable is given to us by our Lord along with many, many others to tell us about the Father. They all tell us the same thing: that we haven't got the slightest notion of the depths of God's mercy. Yet we try to worship some other God. We are still afraid of God when we pray.

In the early centuries when they prayed the Jesus Prayer: "Lord Jesus Christ, Son of the living God, be merciful to me, a sinner," all they were doing was expanding the prayer our Lord described in this parable as justifying. This prayer is not just words. It is something right down in the very depths of a person. There is no bind that I can get myself into that God could ignore and not have mercy on me. We are supposed to realize this. The reason why we repeat this prayer is to remind ourselves of what is really going on. It may be that by some disposition of God's providence we don't back ourselves into a lifetime bind like this crook, with no human way out. This is not important.

The deep reality concerned is a daily affair. Our Lord's spirituality is not abstract. What a tragedy it would be if day by day we did not know the mercy of God. What a tragedy if, not having to experience this kind of bind like this tax collector, we didn't respond to our heavenly Father. What a tragedy if we didn't know that it is not our virtue that makes a difference, but his mercy. This is why people say the Jesus Prayer, the "Prayer of the Publican." It keeps them in touch with reality: that we live by the mercy of God.

Nobody knows why this Pharisee practiced all those virtues. Maybe he was scared of God and afraid he was not going to make it. Or perhaps he really thought he was that great. But the man about whom our Lord said, "He went home at rights with God," was the man who simply asked for mercy because he needed it.

I guess what I am trying to say doesn't fit into words. God is a pushover, but that doesn't mean he is soft. It just means that he is God, he is mercy. And this should be the source of any effort we make to love God or to love anyone, or desire anything as a Christian.

Theoretically, we know that we are all in a bind like that crook, but practically we forget it. If in our hearts there is that prayer of the publican, then we possess that joy of knowing that it doesn't make any difference, for whatever we do or try to do is no longer prompted by our need for rewards, safety, or security. It doesn't make any difference: we may suffer from our own sinfulness but we are completely accepted by God. Why did God have mercy on that man? Because he had the right formulas, the right creed, or said the right thing? No. But because he was in such a bind that he had to ask for mercy, and it was God's delight to accept him fully.

Luke 19: 1-10   *ZACCHAEUS WAS FOR REAL*

This is a very delightful Gospel in many ways. St. Luke is the champion of the down-and-outer. Only he mentions the good thief, Mary Magdalen, the small-time ward boss and politician, Zacchaeus. The Roman rite uses this Gospel at the dedication of a church. No place is a church or is holy until Christ comes to live there. The consecration of anything comes about not through any formula or blessing, but through the presence of Christ, the Word who is present in everything.

I remember an Eastern-rite priest, a friend of mine, who bought a candy dish to use at the liturgy. I asked him if he was going to bless it. He said, "I think the Body of Christ will bless it."

So this fellow Zacchaeus made a fool of himself by climbing up a sycamore tree to see Jesus. Imagine, this wealthy ward boss climbing up a tree! And the Lord, as he passed by, said, "Zacchaeus, make haste and come down, for I must stay at your house today." And so he made haste, came down, and welcomed him with joy. And everybody said, "Look at that, he's going to that sinner's house, Zacchaeus." Zacchaeus said to Jesus, "Lord, half of my goods I give to the poor; if I have wronged anyone, I will restore it fourfold" (The "if" implies a few shady deals!) Our Lord said, "Today salvation has come to this house. The Son of Man came to seek and to save that which was lost."

Christians are sort of professional holy people. We're all supposed to try and become holy. That's a very good idea. But perhaps we are doing with our lives something of what I wanted to do with that candy dish. Are we trying to become holy through some kind of external blessing instead of actually carrying in us the Body of Christ?

St. Paul tells us, "Don't you know that you are the temple of God?" Suppose that we wanted to have a dedication of the temple of our whole being, how would it be made holy? By the presence of Christ.

When we baptize someone we give them the life of Christ. But do we *give* it to them, really? Isn't it rather a matter of freeing something deep within the being of that person, something that could never be set free without an act of Christ? We are supposed to baptize the world, bring Christ to the world. Does it mean that we go and pour Christianity over it, or rather that we, with faith and reverence, call forth the hidden Word, the Christ who is already there? The more present that Christ is anywhere, the holier is the whole of reality.

When Jesus passes by we should make the greatest haste and come down, not worrying about whether we were right or wrong in climbing the tree. After all, if Zacchaeus hadn't done such a thing, if he hadn't been up that high, the Lord would not have noticed him.

Imagine looking for Jesus by climbing a tree! But he did what he could, and our Lord blessed him and made his house holy because he, Jesus Christ, simply was present in it.

Christ is present in us right now by the power, the reality of his holy Spirit, so that if right now we want to be holy, if we want all of our relationships to be holy, all our desires to be holy, then we should make haste and come down and open the very depth of our own being to the Spirit of God, so that who we are becomes a temple of the living God. In such a temple are real hymns of praise being sent up to God, where real sacrifice is being offered for ourselves and for all people.

Why did Jesus pick Zacchaeus, the little ward boss, the little tax collector, the cheap little politician? Maybe because he was *real.* He wanted to see Jesus so badly that he climbed a tree and didn't care what others thought. When Jesus entered his life he gave away half of what he owned. Such a choice cuts through all our ideas of piety and holiness and appropriateness and reveals itself as such a great, beautiful, and light-filled thing.

If we now want to consecrate ourselves we have only to open the door to Christ. When he comes to your home, you will become a temple, a church, a place where man can meet God and God can meet man. A place where God is praised and man is consoled. Then, having a house and a home makes sense because they are holy. It is now a place where man can sing in joy to his Father because Christ is present.

It is significant that the Church's liturgical year, which begins with Advent and the theme of expectation, opens, not with an account of the Annunciation or of our Lord's birth, but with an eschatological prophecy. For the Church does not "make believe" in the liturgy. We are not meant to "pretend" that Jesus is not yet born in Bethlehem. We are meant to understand our own state in the light of what God has done once and for all in Christ. We commemorate the birth of Christ as we live out our own expectancy, awaiting the full manifestation of the glory of the Risen Christ. This commemoration brings with it the special grace caused in this world by the birth and infancy of the Savior.

The three synoptic Gospels all place a discourse (in which our Lord speaks at once of the fall of Jerusalem and the end of all human history) just before their account of the Passion and Resurrection. It is as though before Jesus quits this kind of cosmic existence in the act which we call death, and passes to a new kind of existence which enshrines and transforms all that is human and which we call resurrection, he must state the universal application of the reality which he at once introduces and submits to.

In language borrowed from the classical Hebrew tradition, Jesus describes the End. But he tells us that when these things happen we are to lift up our heads in hope because our redemption is at hand. And this is the paradox of Advent and of all Christian expectation. We must look beyond what we see, but we cannot despise it. We must relinquish our anxious grasp on this world and our need to wrest security from it; but we look forward to that moment when all that the world really means will be radiant, reflecting the light that is on the face of Christ Jesus.

It is at the very time when the cosmos, or our own little share in its life and rhythm, is crashing in seeming confusion, that hope becomes real and our redemption is at hand. We must love this world so well, we must love persons so deeply, that we allow the fire of that love to bring us through the experience of dying to our attachment to them, in order to bring them and us into the light of an eternal life in God. This act is accomplished in a particular way in bodily death, but daily we die, carrying about in our bodies the dying of Jesus so that the life of Jesus may shine forth.

Men today are longing for a transformed cosmos, a world free from suffering and injustice, a great human family where every man is accorded his personal dignity by men he knows to be his brothers. But their efforts, our efforts, are stifled, not only by the enormity of the task but also by an uncertainty as to its ultimate meaning.

How can we commit ourselves to a world which seems forever subjected to vanity? Our Lord's words are meant to convey an answer. Our optimism and our energy draw their life from a reality outside this world which is yet deeply within it. It is the Risen Christ. We can work and weep for the transformation of man's world because we know that it has been accomplished in Christ and must now be extended to our brothers. The power of Christ's love urges us on, not to a problemless security or to a this-world grand success (if this were so, we of all men are the most to be pitied). Rather, we are called to be open to the reality of our existence so that we experience the power of the forces which are even now at work, transforming death into life. "To know the power of his Resurrection, and communion in his sufferings, in being conformed to his death" (Phil 3:10). The accent here is on *his* death.

The night is far advanced, the day is close at hand. The Christian stands with everyone else in the dark, enduring the sufferings of this life, and sharing men's longings. Yet he sees the dawn on the horizon. He has the promise, the certitude of the breaking of the day. He sees the first flush of dawn and says to his brother, "Look, the light is coming! It is somehow already here!" His brother may reply, "I can't see anything." The Christian must be able to answer, "Look here, and see it in my eyes." "Lift up your heads, your redemption is close at hand."

John 1: 43-51   ICON OF THE FATHER

The heroes of our faith, such as are described for example in the Letter to the Hebrews, only saw an image of what they were promised. They wandered about the world so preoccupied with the promises of God that they were as strangers on earth. These people could only salute the City from afar. They knew that they were strangers. God left it that way. Perfection could not be reached until the final age of the world dawned in Christ.

We, in many ways, live in a world of images. Everything speaks of something else. The sun is an image of Christ. The rainbow a reminder of the covenant. But there is one image which doesn't speak of anything beyond—it simply is. And that image is our Lord Jesus Christ. He is the image of the Father by whom he is.

In this Gospel there is stated the question which all disciples ask of Christ sooner or later: "Where do you live?" What we are really asking is, "Is there anything stable? Is there anything that speaks to me directly, anything I don't have to go beyond? Am I too still wandering, saluting the City from afar?"

And our Lord says, "Come and see." He himself is
the Icon of God in the very depth of his being. He is not
someone who is just another image like the sun, the water,
or the trees. He simply *is*, and he is the one image abiding,
who is not fleeting, not changing. He is not sent to all of us
only to vanish again. He *is*.

The mystery of the Icon of God is that this total
selflessness in which Jesus Christ revealed the Father is
exactly what makes him who he is. He is precisely who he
is because he is completely absorbed and preoccupied
with the Father, and so his selflessness is his stability, his
changelessness.

The pace at which life forces us to move creates in us
a deep sense that no matter what it is, it is going to change.
No matter how stable it seems, it is only an image of
something else, and therefore I can't get too involved. I
can't get too settled down in it because it is going to move.
It is not all that it seems to be. It is an image of something
else.

The Icon of the Father, Jesus, doesn't change. He is
not a fleeting image. He is the Son of the living God. Now
we can ask Jesus Christ if he is abiding, if he is stable, or
whether he is just one more fleeting image. His answer to
us is, "Come and see." It means: "Live with me. . .
come. . .see. . .pray with me."

By this "coming and seeing" we know that the Son of
God in his very reality is the Icon. He is the image of God
and he holds the whole world in existence. It is he who
gives everything its consistency. As the Letter to the
Hebrews says, "He is the image of the splendor of God in
whom all things hold together."

But we too are images of God insofar as we resemble
Christ who is *the* image of the Father. We yearn also to be
stable. We really want to be eternal and last forever, to be

something that is not just fleeting, an illusion that passes and never abides. If we are as completely absorbed in Christ as Christ is with the Father, then we are also stable. We are not an illusion to ourselves or to anyone else. In the reality of becoming an image of Jesus, we find out who we are.

All this may sound very abstract, but I am deeply convinced it is true, and that it is part of the Gospel. All I can say to myself and to everyone else is what Philip said to Nathaniel. Nathaniel said, "Can anything good come out of Nazareth?" In other words, "Is this, can this be true? It is nice to think about and to hope for, but is it really so? Can it be the solution we have been saluting from afar? It sounds wonderful, Philip, but is it true—can anything *that* good come out of Nazareth?" And Philip simply answered, "Come and see."

With the world forcing us to move so fast, we all seem to be living on an express train—without a conductor! Things just fly by, and nothing seems to last for very long. But one of our deepest needs is for something stable, something lasting. That stability is our Lord Jesus Christ, because he is the Icon who is never-changing, who is not an image of something else, but is an image of the Father *by being who he is.* We will know this if we "come and see." Orthodoxy does not consist then in thinking thoughts that correspond to formulas, but in "abiding with Christ" and knowing that he is the only Word who expresses God.

John 2: 1-11   *LONGING IS PRESENCE*

There are so many aspects to this Gospel, mostly I suppose, because John has the capacity to write on so many levels at once. John intends us to see in this incident a revelation of the glory of Christ, the response to which is faith. And it is upon that note that the incident ends.

The wedding feast at Cana initiates the public life of our Lord, just as his glorification on the cross ends it. We find our Lady present at both incidents, and in both places she is addressed as "woman." Here we have water and wine, and there we see water and blood. Cana is the first sign and Jesus is revealed in his glory. Calvary is the last sign where Jesus is glorified because by his life he has glorified the Father.

The statement of the Mother of Jesus sums up in a way the longing and deficiencies of man: "they have no wine." This statement of Christ's Mother must have gone deeply into his heart. Rather than say, "Isn't it too bad, Mother, I really wish we could do something," Jesus must have seen this request as a sign from his Father. He must have realized that the time had come to initiate that process which would result in his "hour." His Mother must have seen this registered in his eyes, and she said to the waiters, "Do whatever he tells you."

We have no wine either. We have nothing which can rejoice the heart of man, so to speak. We have nothing like God's gift of wine. We have only water to bring to him, and by a glance he can change it into wine. How long will we hesitate before bringing our water to Christ? How long before we will know the taste of God's wine?

There is still much in us that is "water." The Spirit of God has not taken complete hold of our hearts yet. We experience what is lacking in our humanity and in the world. As the continuation of Christ in the world, we are meant somehow to continue the reality of Christ's saving power by turning the water of men's desires, men's longings, into the wine of fulfillment.

We live in the era of history characterized by the sacraments. That is to say, we live in that period between the "already accomplished" in the passion and resurrection, and the "not yet;" we wait now for the full manifestation of Christ in glory. We long for something which is somehow present and available but which we do not possess entirely.

We cry out to God, and in the depths of that cry we find God himself. It is not that God comes from someplace else, but that he is found within the depths of that cry. The very fact that we are longing for God is a sign of the presence of God. Until we behold Christ, it can be no other way. Yet there are times when our longing itself becomes a source of joy. We can stifle this longing, this awareness of our poverty, as being nothing but tasteless water. We'll probably make it to heaven, but without ever knowing what it is to live by wine; others will never know either.

As disciples, we have firsthand experience of what it is to be water before God. But if we persevere in prayer, we will have the experience of knowing that the glance of Christ can change the very depths of our being into the wine of joy. That experience of the power of Christ, which is born of the experience of our own weakness, is the source of compassion, love, and kindness. And through it other men may then experience what it is to have their water changed into wine by the glance of Christ in us and through us. And then men will see that for which they have longed in the very depths of their beings.

The Christian experience is a source of power, and it is accomplished in water and blood. Baptism and Eucharist, consecration and passion. We must all bring our water to Christ so that he can change us into wine. Our wine then can be a source of joy to men.

Hardly anywhere in the Gospels do we see such a clear picture of Jesus the Prophet. Not only does our Lord (in words which are obviously colored by the words of Jeremiah, Isaiah, and the great prophets) foretell the future destruction of his city but, in the prophetic tradition, he weeps over his people while he burns with anger at their blind refusal to accept the proffered gift of salvation.

After having wept and prayed, Jesus acts: he walks into his Father's house and he makes a mess of it. He drives people out saying that they have turned it into a robber's den. Again he says, "My house shall be a house of prayer." But paradoxically we also read, "He was daily teaching in the temple." Why didn't he leave? Why did he continue to go there, to the "robber's den"?

As with nearly every other story in the Gospel there are two facets to it. One is our Lord's relationship to us, and the other is our relationship with mankind right now. We are told in the documents of the Vatican council that the people of God are a priestly people, a royal race, a living prophecy. And here, in this Gospel, we see what it is to be a prophet.

Our Lord was in love with his own city. At the thought of what would become of it because of its rejection of him, he was moved to tears. The man who drove off the people with rage at what he saw is the same Jesus who so loved Jerusalem that he wept. The man who denounced all the abominations perpetrated in his Father's house, that same man also stayed there and taught daily in that temple.

We often talk glibly about tears for the world. We often talk about an apostle as mediator. Well, here is a picture of what a mediator looks like. He is someone who is so joined to those who are disunited that in himself he feels the tension of their separation. No man can do for Jerusalem what Christ has done unless that person loves the city and weeps over it and for it.

And no man can weep unless he is willing to act. No man can act unless he is willing to stay. No man has the right to try and reform anything unless he is willing to stay in the place of division. Our Lord was a strong person. He was not light-hearted or sentimental. And yet he wept. He wept because he loved his city, Jerusalem. He saw the shortsightedness, the smallmindedness of its inhabitants. He saw the fear of risk that kept its people captive so that they could neither see nor enter upon the way that led to true peace.

Now all these things were written for our instruction. Not only do we have a great responsibility to live out the prophetic aspect of our baptism (which means to weep, act, and stay), but we have to accept Christ's own activity in our regard.

There is something admittedly terrible about imagining Christ standing in that temple and driving those people out, something that fills us with terror. But think of our Lord's weeping. Think of his weeping over us. That's how much he loved us. The thought comes to me that we are the temple of God. We are the house of prayer. The buildings that we are are the temples which Christ enters. In every one of us there is at least some corner where people are trading. There is some spot in us that is not a house of prayer. What right do we have to drive anyone out of God's larger temple, the Church, even in righteous anger, unless we are willing to let the tears and the strength of Christ drive some of the "buying and selling" out of our own hearts?

We should all pray for God's holy people, the new Jerusalem, over whom we too are meant to shed tears.

There can be no final end to this Jerusalem; we have Christ's word for it. The question is, does this people of God know at this moment what it must do for its peace? Does it know the way? We are that Church. If we could allow the tears and strength of Christ to drive some of the buying and selling out of us, then we too would be a house of prayer. If we know this experience because we receive it from Christ, then we know the strength that comes from compassion and the tenderness that comes with anger. Then we too will stay with mankind.

"Staying with mankind" does not mean mere juxtaposition with other humans. Presence is not a question of mere geographical location. It's a matter of intensity, of caring enough to weep.

I don't have to go on to describe the confusion, the fear, the smallmindedness, the intellectual arrogance that is holding the holy people of God back from really being the temple of God, the house of prayer. I know it's true because it's in me, and you know it because it's in you. If this word of God is to be effective in us, then today, before the sun goes down, the people of God must become more of a house of prayer. There is no other possible response to this Gospel. We should be ready to weep then, not for the people but with the people, and we should have the guts to act and to stay.

John 3: 13-17   *LITTLE SOULS JUST GET WET*

Our greatest problem is trying to justify the cross. Every time we try to talk about the lightness of the cross, we talk about the fruits of the cross. Through the cross we somehow come to understand that we don't have to be afraid of death and suffering, of fear and loneliness, that this is the temple where we meet Christ.

On the other hand, every time we think about or experience suffering we are afraid, and that's only natural. We realize that between ourselves and the vision of God there is pain; we are afraid. But the one thing we tend to forget is that in pain there is Christ. We may not understand this, but in some way we experience that it is true. The Church also gives us many examples of saints who have experienced this truth much more than we, and she offers them for our meditation.

St. Theresa of Avila knew such joys in union with Christ that she said, "Let me suffer or die." In other words, "Let me be here in the joy of union with Christ, or let me go to see Him. Only don't let me waste any more precious time in looking for strength or consolation."

Or look at St. Francis of Assisi, scandalizing the people around him because as he lay dying he couldn't stop singing, despite the wounds in his hands and feet. As he lay there, his body wasted, partly isolated from the very group he had founded, he composed the last line of his beautiful hymn to the sun. It was a verse in honor of his sister, joy.

In the mystery of pain there is also the mystery of moving with Jesus. When we are in pain with him we also experience that our flesh is in union with him, and we begin to understand a little better the words of St. Paul: "I don't want to know anything except Jesus Christ and the power of his Resurrection, and being conformed to his death, to his suffering, the image of his suffering."

Through the power of the cross we experience that the power of the resurrection is stronger than the power of death.

There is a lovely story about St. Polycarp. He was a martyr of the early Church. When they tied him to a stake and started to burn all the wood around him, Polycarp began to pray, and the prayer that he prayed is really like a

Canon of a Mass. Now he doesn't need bread and wine, because he himself is the victim. Now the Holy Spirit is transforming the body and blood of Polycarp into the Body and Blood of Christ. The Eucharist now reaches its full fruition, because Polycarp is perfectly united with Christ in the offering.

St. Therese of the Child Jesus was also a great saint, one in whom the glory of the passion of Christ was fully revealed. Once she said: "When there is pain and trials in life, great souls soar on their wings high above the clouds, where everything is so calm and peaceful and the sun is shining. Little souls just stand there and get wet."

It's a curious thing that some souls seemed to be more heroic in the face of suffering than Jesus was. St. John de Brebeuf opened his arms as they cut out his heart. He was in ecstasy because the Lord somehow made John more impressive in suffering than Jesus was himself. Jesus was afraid when he suffered.

Perhaps he wanted to reveal to us the surpassing power of the resurrection. These saints, and the whole body of believers, have witnessed in their lives to the mystery of joy in suffering. In the little bit of pain that we have to suffer, we know it too.

The "lifting up" of Jesus in this Gospel is the lifting up on the cross. Let us not be afraid to look up at that blinding center of light which is so bright that it looks like darkness to us. Weak though he was, and in pain though he was, and afraid though he was, he was transformed by the power of the Holy Spirit. Now he is alive and his suffering shines. He died and rose that our faith too might be strong enough to see joy in the midst of suffering.

John 4: 5-42   *GOD'S WILL IS OUR MEASURE*

We might be astonished to hear our Lord reveal

himself so completely to this woman who had five husbands and who casually meets him because she went to draw water while he was tired and sitting at the well. We hear all her very inept questions to his statements when he promises her living water—"You haven't even got a bucket!" And yet, for the first time in this Gospel, Jesus says openly to the woman, "I am the Messiah. I am the one you are looking for."

This story has a great deal to do with the notion of truth. Jesus refers to himself in the context of the discussion about worshipping in "spirit and in truth." To worship God in spirit and in truth is to worship God in and through Christ. Truth is not a static thing. The truth in which we worshipped God last year, or last week, is not the truth in which we worship God today. If we have been open to the truth, we are in the process of being transformed. Thus to worship God in spirit and in truth is to know God more deeply every day.

This is to say, "God's truth, not ours," The greatest arrogance we exercise in regard to God is to approach him with our truth and impose it on God. We try to measure our growth in spirit and in truth by our notions of spirit and truth. God's will is our measure, and his will is that we keep his commandments. Only then do we abide in his love. He who abides in the love of Christ lives in the truth and the truth makes him free.

Our temptation today is that while we esteem the things of man, we don't love them enough, we don't love them as God loves them. The Son of God came and gave us the living waters of his own blood. Jesus is alive, and he himself is the source of living waters in our hearts. For us to worship in spirit and in truth is to allow ourselves to be transformed into light.

Thus the spirit and truth in which we worshipped yesterday isn't enough for today, because God loves us and

God is transforming everything into Christ. If we know this love of God, that he loved the world so much that he sent his only begotten Son, then we can "let go." God loves and cherishes man. He is the lover of men. But with our arrogance and stupidity and our frantic clinging to things, we stop that process by which God and his great love is transforming everything into life and beauty forever. To move in and with this transforming spirit is to be a pilgrim.

A pilgrim is someone who is always moving—but toward God. And that is to worship in spirit and truth. This is the truth that sets us free. There isn't any great or noble or beautiful desire for which we yearn in our hearts which God doesn't know about, which God doesn't love, which God doesn't cherish and make live forever. This is the optimism of worshipping in truth: God loves us.

We are free because God cares. We are free because Jesus Christ died and rose. Therefore, our greatest temptation is against faith. Not faith as a proposition in our heads, but as a living reality, that faith by which we know God, and know that he is transforming everything into life forever. It is not enough to stop at aggiornamento either in the life of the Church or in our own life. We cannot stop until we are at the parousia.

We don't have to worship on this mountain or on that mountain, but we do have to worship in spirit and in truth. We should pray for the whole Church that it allows the Spirit of Truth to have full freedom in its life. Neither is it a matter of gritting our teeth and allowing the Spirit to do violence to us, as if He were moving against everything we really are. But we submit to his action in the faith that God is transforming us, that he loves us, and that all we truly are will be alive forever. Then we experience that all we truly are will be alive forever. Then we experience that spring of living water which wells up unto life eternal.

"This is my body which is for you.". . ."This is my body which will be given up for you.". . ."This is my body which will be broken for you." All of these are modifications of the words of the Lord when he gave us his body and his blood.

Our Lord said that his flesh was real food, his blood was real drink. The mysteriousness of this body which is the Eucharist is a symbol of the fact that in Christ all dreams come true. Everything that we dream and yearn for in the depth of our soul has substance. It all takes on a tangible dimension in Jesus Christ. There is no make-believe with Christ. He doesn't say, "I'd like to be with you. I'd really like to have you draw your very life from me. So think about me once in a while. Think hard about my birth, my example, and perhaps you will be somewhat inspired."

No. He says, "This is my body. Here it is for *you.* Here is my blood, here, drink it. . .it is for you." Even now, in this life, we live by God. Even now, in this life, where we still need to eat and drink, the most substantial food we have is the body and blood of Jesus. There is no make-believe with Jesus, no wishful thinking, no dream-like pie-in-the-sky. So there can be no make-believe with us either. We must also say to God, "This is my body which is for you. This is my blood which I have given up for you." Just as Jesus did not mean his gift in any purely metaphorical sense, so neither can we simply make-believe in our self-giving.

The mystery of the Eucharist is that in Jesus everything takes on substance and form. The glorious thing is that even who and what we desire to be in the depths of our hearts, even this is not mere wishful thinking. It is real, it really happens. We're baptized to be the sign of the presence of God in the world, because we live in Christ.

This sign does not happen because we speak eloquently or think quickly or sing well or can organize an apostolate or do any other great thing. It is too real to depend on mere human actions. It takes place right in our flesh and blood or it doesn't take place at all. Our religion is not a very spiritual religion in that sense. We take reality seriously. We realize just how seriously when we reflect on this mystery of the body and blood of Christ. Our faith says that it is not an unfortunate situation to be human. Being human is not an obstacle to being spiritual. Being human is the very stuff, the very sacrament by which we touch and radiate God.

If we want to be truly human then we have to say to God, "This is my body which is for you." If we are really transformed, this gift of ourselves cannot be a mere dream or just an idea. St. Paul reminds us that when we come to receive the Eucharist we should examine ourselves whether or not we have been the cause of schism in the community or failed to take care of the poor. If you are guilty of any of those things, he says, you have failed to discern the body of Christ. The body of Christ is the community of the world. We ourselves truly become the body of Christ when all that the Eucharist stands for really exists in us.

If we move in the power of the Spirit who transforms this body and blood, then we'll be truly spiritual, because we will be transformed by the Spirit of God. Then everything we dream about will really be present. People are consoled. Tears stop. People smile. Eyes start to light up. People are coming to know God.

Let us praise the Father who moved our Lord to give us his body and blood. Jesus could hardly wait for that moment. Let us too have this longing of Christ to be burned up, used, eaten up, consumed for the glory of God and for the consolation of all men. Then we will truly be celebrating the mystery of the Body of Christ.

John 8: 31-47   *CHRIST THE ABIDING ONE*

This Gospel highlights the tension between Jesus and the Jews. It is meant to give us a profound understanding of what is going to transpire at the Passion and Resurrection. This Gospel is the last of three dialogues which begin very early in chapter 7. We find in these last three dialogues a three-fold use of the phrase "I am." "When you have raised up the Son of Man then you will know that I am." "You do not believe that I am." "Before Abraham was, I am."

In this last dialogue we find the contrast between Jesus and his relationship to the Father and to Abraham on the one hand, and on the other hand the relationship of the Jews to Abraham and to the Father, whom they call God although they do not know him. We are told, "If you abide in my Word, then you are truly my disciples, and you will know the truth, and the truth will make you free." Here, Our Lord says, "If any man keep my Word, he will never die." The Jews answer, "What do you mean, we will never die? Abraham is dead, the prophets are dead. What do you mean when you use the words 'a man will never die'?"

The death about which Jesus is speaking is the death of separation from God. Those who keep the Word of Christ—those who believe in him—keep the Word of God and believe in the Father; therefore they are alive and not dead. They live a life, the life of Christ, and this, once begun, goes on forever. There will never be a moment in which we are not conscious. Our eternity has begun and our abiding in the Word will one day flower into an eternal vision. We are now in faith what we will be forever. . . children of the living God. This capacity to worship the living God, which is the glory of the Hebrews, is, in its depths, the capacity to love, to adore, to receive him as children receive their father.

So before the Passion begins we are given an insight into the meaning of the redemption: the humiliation, the rejection, crucifixion and resurrection of Christ. The Church places squarely before us the death of Jesus Christ. This Jesus who is going to die and rise and show forth the glory of God, is precisely that infinite Person who, because he dwells in the Father's love, is one with the Father. If we abide in the word of Christ we are no longer slaves of sin, we are free because the truth makes us free. We are alive with the Spirit of Truth.

Throughout our lives, this is the source of our joy. Notice that Our Lord does not say that we must cling to this reality frantically, but rather that we must abide in it. To abide is simply to refuse to go someplace else. To abide is to refuse to be forced or drawn out of the Word of God. The Word of Christ is for us, as it were, an atmosphere, and if we abide in it, it draws us into the mystery of Christ.

Who is it that is going to die and rise again? God. The very Son of God. Our faith accepts this but the rest of our being falters before it. We don't really understand what is happening because we don't really understand this witnessing through Our Lord and the Word by which He witnesses to Himself. Abraham began to be, all men began, but Jesus *is*. If we abide in this Word of Christ who is, then we allow all of reality into ourselves, and then we are free because the truth makes us free. We are starved for the truth. The body and blood of Christ are precisely the body and blood of the truth, and upon this we feed. Christ said, "I am the truth," and he died to make us free. The reality of Christ is what frees us from the only thing which enslaves us: sin.

There are many things we must pray about, many things we must do as we approach this re-presentation, this calling to mind of the Passion and Resurrection. But the foundation of all that activity consists in an openness to the spirit in which we live. His power draws us into an understanding of who Christ is, recalling to our mind all that he said and did. Left to ourselves we cannot see because we are blind. But Christ exercises a freeing activity upon us by allowing us to touch the well-springs of his soul.

Many verses of the psalms come to mind in this context because Christ prayed them. "My God, my God, why have you abandoned me?" These are expressions of the truth because they are expressions of Christ. The depth out of which they proceed is that joy, that light, that fire of love which binds the Father and the Son, and it is that depth which when we see it, when we enter into it and when we abide in it, makes us free. For nothing is fully Christian until it frees us and no experience is fully Christian until it brings us joy.

So then as we meditate on this Gospel, we hear Christ saying to us, "I am." Not "I began to be," or "I will be," or "I will come to be," but "I am." He is the abiding One. In this reality we know the freedom of being in touch with that dynamic reality which is the Passion and Resurrection, and experience within ourselves the joy and the light which bear witness within us to the truth.

John 9: 1-12   *LOSING IS FINDING*

This Gospel, in the wisdom of the Church, is meant

to make us concentrate on what is really essential in our conversion, our metanoia. We often think of "penance" as giving up something or other, and it is a good thing. But we could give away everything we have, and if we have no love, it is nothing. We could burn our bodies in protest against a war, but without love it would be of no value. We could read all the spiritual books in the public library, but without love it would be nothing at all.

We know, as St. Paul tells us, that unless we grow in love, we are nothing. Unless we are the salt of the earth, we are nothing. If most of us think love is so important, how do we go about getting in on it? I'm sure we will all agree it is not easy. We try to control our emotions and our tempers, but it isn't easy to be nice to everyone. But there is more to love than just controlling ourselves.

In all of the Gospels, one of the predictions of the Passion is linked with the healing of this blind man before Jericho. Christ sets off for Jerusalem in what St. Luke calls his "exodus." St. John talks about the vocation of the Son of Man and thus, in some ways, is talking about our own vocations. On his way our Lord meets a blind man and by His word, gives that man his sight.

We are the Son of Man, but we are also the blind man, and what Christ has done for us by touching us and giving us sight, we must do for the world. There are three things: faith, hope and love, but the greatest of these is love because it lasts forever. Somehow, we are to suffer and rise, and this gives people sight: they can see God in us.

That this is the intention of the Evangelists in placing the prediction of the Passion and the curing of the blind man side by side, there is no doubt. As St. Luke says, something of Christ gives this man sight—his very spittle. You may wonder whether or not something that you are suffering means anything. Don't look at it in terms of practicality or usefulness, that is, whether or not it is helping you to grow in virtue and holiness. The mystery lies in this, that something of you, something of Christ, touches somebody somewhere. It may happen, and probably will. It may happen in your life or in mine. We may know someone who touched us, or whom we touched, and now can see.

There are people all over the world who will never know us, yet they will "see" somehow if we, as Christ, yearn to fulfill the vocation of the Son of Man. That is the meaning of our life. We are looking for meaning in our lives and we should. We will look for something to give meaning to our lives day in and day out. This vocation of the Son of Man does happen every day and it gives somebody light. Our Lord said that he looked forward to this great event in his life when he would die and rise again. He could only be joyful at the prospect because he possessed that love of which St. Paul speaks. Some at least saw that the power which Christ exercised in conveying sight upon this man derived from the Passion. Such healing by Christ is the foreshadowing of the great saving act of the Cross and Resurrection, and a symbol of the Church's vocation.

That event is now already existing. It really transpires in us. It is the power of Christ which gives sense to our lives. This is supposed to give us joy, but it will only give us joy when we really love. The thought of other people having sight is our consolation, but is only our consolation if we love. Does that mean we have to stir ourselves up and really love? No, we just have to get out of the way and let this power in us, given by Christ, come to fulfillment.

Life seems to consist in a successive losing of the very thing we think is holding us together. This process continues until we find that it is God who gives us our consistency, holds us in being and in Christ. Therefore, as we go through life we have to find something that holds us together, but every day we lose something that we think we need for this! If we can learn that this kind of dying, this kind of "losing" is our vocation, we will know what joy is.

We are made to know the joy of giving others sight. In the Eastern Rite this Gospel is used for the preparation of Baptism; Baptism in the East is called Enlightenment. Our vocation through Baptism is to enter evermore deeply with Christ into the mystery of his Death and Resurrection. And this daily dying means something. It means that somewhere somebody will receive his sight. And once in a while this will thrill you, to know that the power in us can give sight to men all over the world.

John 10: 22-30   *THE GIFT OF CHRIST'S LOVE*

We have in this passage a mysterious blending of themes that run all through St. John's Gospel. While they are sometimes difficult to follow, they are worth dwelling upon, since they are the Word of God and show us the true state of things.

Our Lord is the Good Shepherd whom we see in the song of the psalmist, "The Lord is my shepherd." He is also the Shepherd King about whom Ezechial and Jeremiah wrote. He is the Shepherd who, in the book of Wisdom, leads the flocks of Israel. Our Lord said that he was the Good Shepherd, just as he said that he was the true vine.

Jesus also said that our relationship to him is one of mutual knowledge and love. He knows us and we know him, just as he knows the Father and the Father knows him.

As the passage continues in the Gospel, it shows us that the knowledge by which Christ knows the Father comes to its complete expression in that act by which he lays down his life for his sheep, for this is what his Father commands. We understand what a shepherd is in this action. It is the understanding of mutual love and knowledge by which the will of God the Father actually exists. His will is done. Christ says that we know him as the Good Shepherd because he lays down his life for us. St. John in his first letter draws the same conclusion: "Brethren, we know his love in that he laid down his life for us;" we too should give our lives for one another.

If the only commandment Christ gave us was that we love one another and give our lives for one another, the reason is that this is the commandment of the Father. Our Lord kept it himself and gave his life for us; thus he actually existed as the Good Shepherd. There is no such thing as obedience in the Christian life: obedience in the sense of following a norm or an order. There is only one commandment, and that is that the will of God be done. This commandment of God exists insofar as we love one another and lay down our life for all men in the world. This act flows from our knowledge of Christ and leads to it.

So we know Christ and are known by him as he knows the Father. This knowledge that Christ has in knowing the Father he gives to us, and we are meant to give it to the whole world. That act by which we give is an act of love. There is, therefore, only one commandment which, paradoxically enough, cannot be commanded. If it is forced, it isn't love.

The only commandment we have from God is love, and this love he continues to make visible in the world. Sometimes we feel that we are far from such love, that we are "out of it," and that it doesn't seem to change the world. But the truth is that this love isn't something we create within ourselves. All we can do is be aware of this reality that Christ has brought us and that we have in abundance. This is the truth, regardless of whether or not this reality brings us emotional reactions. It's true. The relationship between the Father and Son is our relationship with Jesus Christ.

St. Peter defines it well when he says that "we love him whom we have not seen." One of the greatest things from which we must detach ourselves is *our idea* of love. We hear we must allow Christ's love to dwell in us—then we use *our* idea of love to discourage ourselves and convince ourselves that we do not possess any love! We should hold fast to the description of love which Jesus has given us in this holy Word of God. If we go to Jesus simply, knowing how unlike this reality we are—and yet going constantly to the Good Shepherd—we too will realize and experience his gift to us, because we are on the way to Christ who is the truth.

John 14: 18-31   *THE POETRY OF GOD*

Pentecost is the completion of the work of Christ, his gift of the Spirit. This Gospel passage is taken from a section of St. John where our Lord is answering the question of Judas (not the Iscariot), "How is it that you will reveal yourself to us and not to the world?" Jesus answered, "If anyone loves me he will keep my word."

Pentecost is the day when Christ sends his Spirit. The Spirit who reaches from end to end sweetly and orders all things with strength is the greatest access we have to the omnipotence of God.

If we look into the lives of the saints, of the apostles, we see as they saw, that the transformation effected in them was done through the Holy Spirit of God. The Spirit of the Lord, the wind of God, the fire of God, the water of God. Our Lord tells us that when the breeze blows we know that it is present but we have no idea where it comes from or where it is going. We are unable to start or stop the breeze of God. The Spirit, like the wind, is not under the control of man.

At the very creation of this world, as the Bible portrays for us, there was chaos, lying inert, unable to respond to God. There was waste and void and the Spirit of God hovered over the water. When the Hebrews left Egypt, God spread his wings over them like an eagle's. When God personally intervened in the Incarnation, there was the over-shadowing of the Holy Spirit. The Spirit, in whom we believe, is the life-giver, One with the Father and the Son; he spoke through the prophets.

Each day can be a pentecost for us if we open to this breeze which is the Spirit. We cannot start this breeze, nor can we stop it. But we can render it, in our own regard, as nothing more than an illusion, as a mere passing experience. Yes, we can say no to the life-giver, the Spirit of God who is over-shadowing us at this very moment.

But when we are open to him he does wondrous things. He puts order in chaos, fashions a temple in the womb of a Virgin, and unites men with God. When we are open to this Spirit something very deep in man is satisfied, his creaturehood. Man is then able to see the artistry of God, the poetry of God, the suppleness of God, in this Spirit of love.

Were it not for this Spirit, the urging of Christ in the Gospel could be nothing more than a technique instead of the art it is under the Spirit's inspiration. I say that he reveals the poetry of God to us because though he is a person, we have no name for him. We say "Father," and "Son," but when it comes to the Spirit we speak of wind and breeze and water and fire, because the Spirit is a spirit of love, and we have no words for love.

We need to make of our souls an upper room where we wait. Then the Spirit of God will hover over us, and will, as a breeze, blow through us and we will know the wonderful works of God. And then even our poor words can become as living flames; our very being can be a fire, because this is not the work of chaos or of a nomadic group, but of the Spirit of God.

This contribution of man to await like thirsty soil the rain of God, the dew of God, this waiting itself gives glory to God. Why? Because it testifies to the reality of God as a poet. There are many images which the Fathers of the Church have tried to use to give us a sense of the spiritual, the joyful. One of them is the smile on the face of Christ inspired by the Spirit.

Men today need to know that God is a poet, they need to know that God is Spirit. We need to know it too. We need to know that deep surrendering of the core of our being, so that as Ezechial says, we no longer have a heart of stone but a heart of flesh. Let us pray that we may be touched by the poetry of God, by the smile of Christ. Then we will really be changed. The chaos, the thirsty ground within us, will receive the dew of God.

John 16: 16-28   *WHAT'S IN A NAME?*

One of the themes of the scripture reading is self-awareness. In the letter of James (1:22-25), we read that the true Christian is one who looks into the law of life and freedom and recognizes himself. When he looks into revelation he senses what he is. The man who sees revelation and walks off and forgets is a fool. There is no true realization. The true Christian, understanding who he is, begins to act that way, acting out what he has seen himself to be. He is actively one with himself, and through that oneness begins to understand revelation.

In the Gospel passage we have a discourse of Our Lord on the Church. This is the last part of that chapter, and it ends in an act of faith by the Apostles: "We are certain now that you know everything, and do not need to be questioned; because of this we believe that you have come from God."

As St. John writes this he has the risen Christ standing there amidst the apostles, and Christ says, "Until this moment you have not asked for anything in my name. Ask and you shall receive, and find your joy made perfect. All this I have been telling you in metaphors. The time is coming when I shall speak no more to you in metaphors but will tell you plainly about the Father. When that day comes, you will ask in my name; I do not tell you that I shall pray to the Father for you, for the Father himself loves you, because you love me and believe that I came from God."

What does it mean to ask for something in the name of Christ, as it says in the earlier part of the same Gospel, "Whatever you ask the Father in my name he will give it to you?"

A name is not just a sound. It expresses what a thing really is and what that person really is. To know the name of God in the Old Testament is to have some way of touching God. God forbade Moses and all the Hebrew people to make an image of him, something that could be touched, handled, and controlled. But since man is made to touch and have access to God, he gave them his name.

Anyone who really says "Yahweh" has God present to him. The name "Jesus" expresses that whole person who is "He who has come forth from God." Not come from God as any missionary or prophet, but who came *forth* from God. For a man who says "Jesus" and who really knows what he is saying, already has God present to him.

To ask in the name of Jesus is to ask in Christ. It is to ask, as St. James says, not in words, not because of words, but because of union with Christ, in the expression of who Christ is in the reality of our soul. Our Lord is careful to add that for someone who is related to him in this way, that person has no need to ask Jesus to pray to the Father for him. The Father is in the Son and the Son is in the Father. The very moment that someone prays in the name of Jesus, he has God the Father present, and the Father loves us. As Christ is in the Father and the Father in Christ, so we are in Christ and Christ is in us.

James tells us that for anyone to understand truly God's revelation, he must give it a full human existence, or, in a very biblical phrase, he must not be a "forgetful listener." To put into practice, in the Bible, is simply not to forget. To do is to remember, to know. Someone, then, who allows the message of God, who is Christ, to be the very source of all he does, knows the Father of Jesus. He knows who Christ is, and in so knowing, he prays, and as he prays in the name of Christ, the Father is present and hears this prayer.

It is rare that you hear our Lord add all the qualifications of theology manuals—that it should be according to God's will, etc., etc. He simply says, "Ask *anything* in my name." He says, in effect, "If you are one with me you can ask anything in my name." God is omnipotent and God is merciful, and God can bring all mankind into the body of Christ. God can do that for us. God wants to do that. This is the source of our hope. If then we allow this Spirit of God, this reality of Christ, to be the well-spring of all we think and do, then "ask anything." Since we are in his name, we receive it, and our joy is complete.

James, who is more practically orientated, makes it very clear: the man who hears this word of God has a chance to understand himself, see who he is. If he goes away and allows that vision to be the source of all he is and does, he understands revelation. But God's revelation is not a formula but a person: Christ. The person understands Christ. Then, when he says, "Jesus Christ," he not only knows what he is saying but *who* he is, and already his joy is complete.

Our Lord said that we need not ask the Father because the Father knows and loves us. If we are living in the name of Christ we already have access to the Father. Let us pray then in Jesus' name. We know what we need. Let us take our Lord literally and ask in his name, and we will know the joy Christ speaks of.

John 18: 33-38   THE KINGDOM OF TRUTH

Everyone who belongs to the truth listens to the voice of Christ. Truth for St. John resides in the Father, is given over completely to the Son, and imparted by the Spirit to all who are willing to receive it. Truth is a dynamic reality; it brings things, it brings people, back to the Father.

There once was a man on his way to Rome to be martyred. The influential Roman Christians were all trying to obtain his release, for after all, he was the bishop of Antioch, St. Ignatius. At one point in his letter, as he is trying to dissuade the Christians from depriving him of his chance "to be a disciple," he wrote: "I hear a voice within me, and it's like the sound of running water, and it says to me, 'Come to the Father, Come to the Father.' " That's truth.

Our Lord is King. We recognize it everywhere. All authority is power. The kingdom, the realm of his power, is the truth. We are subjects of this King of truth, and yet, paradoxical as it might sound, he said the truth would make us free! He has told us that he himself is the truth. Truth is a dynamic reality. It is a reality speaking in the depths of our hearts, the sound of this running water which murmurs "Come to the Father." Those who hear this voice beckoning them to the Father are hearing as well, "Come to the truth." Truth is inexorable. We don't refute the truth. It is simply there. We either accept it or reject it, but we always recognize its power.

Looking at the sun coming through a window, it seems to be doing more than merely reflecting light off objects. It seems to be penetrating and permeating all things. Our Lord as the Truth is like that. He is the reality which illuminates from within—he is the Resurrected one, the Christ who is alive.

If we listen to this voice which beckons us to come to the Father, if we allow ourselves to accept the truth, we will see this inexorability of reality. This frightens us, yet somehow it is also kind, somehow it also brings peace. It frightens us as long as we try to stand outside of reality, measure it, "get a handle on" everything. It is only by accepting God on his terms that we experience the depth of things: that we are incomplete, and that God is constantly offering us salvation. If we accept this offer we belong to the truth and we are free. Everything that is, is, and God respects every bit of it. God never "pretends" that something never happened—not even in the case of man's sin. He does not impose salvation from without, but nourishes it from within the very depths of what man has made of his world.

Our Lord came to bear witness to this truth. In some way a Christian witness, a Christ-witness *causes* the reality he is witnessing to. Our Lord came to bear witness to the truth, and he himself is that truth. If we belong to the truth, our very being witnesses to the truth, and somehow we know the strength, the power, the reality, the suffering of the truth. At the same time we know the gentleness, the freedom, the kindness, the power of Jesus Christ working deep within this world, within every soul in this world, within the Church. We hear that voice saying "Come to the Father." The Kingdom of God is not of this world. It is a pure gift from without. And yet, just as a candle stands and is unable of itself to bring forth light, but does bear light once it is touched with fire, so a soul once touched by the fire of Christ, itself now burns from within.

The truth is that Jesus Christ is alive. The truth is that God so loved the world that he gave his Son. The truth is that in this was love known, that he gave his life for us. If we are willing to open ourselves up, if we are willing to listen deeply to this voice, we will know truth, truth in all its ramifications. Painfully but gently it will make us free, and we will be able to say what Christ said, "I came to bear witness to the truth."

John 20: 24-30   THE THOMAS IN US

There is another chapter in this Gospel, but it is more or less an appendix to the total message of St. John. Thus, the last words that we have in the Gospel are these: "These things have been recorded so that you may believe that Jesus is the Christ, the Messiah, the Son of God, and that believing you may have life in his name." Whoever believes in the Son of God possesses God in the depths of his heart, and as St. John says in his first letter, whoever possesses the Son, has life.

The most dramatic aspects of the incident described in this Gospel deal with Thomas, the doubter, and Thomas, the believer. But the essential message of the Gospel has to do with the faith of every Christian. Thomas saw and believed. He saw the Risen Christ and believed that Jesus is Lord and God. In that sense, his faith is not less that ours. The notions of life and belief are joined here by St. John in his use of the word "blessed." Blessedness in the Bible is linked to life, to fruitfulness, and here the believer who does not see is said to possess life.

If the resurrection is a mystery of life, then our access to it is in faith. When we hear a statement like that we instinctively look into ourselves and see so little faith that we are tempted to conclude that we have very little life as well. We say to ourselves, "I am more like Thomas. I have never been able to say either like the other apostles, 'I have seen the Lord.' "

Thomas wanted to put his fingers into the wounds of Christ's hands and to place his hand in the wounded side of Christ. Yet, when he was confronted with the opportunity, he didn't do it. Rather he confessed, "My Lord and My God." It is true that at our conscious level we bear a close resemblance to Thomas in that everything in us wants to see and touch and to be reassured. Our small faith seems to rest on the expectation of such an experience. Yet we are confronted here with a blessing pronounced on those who do not see, but believe. We desire the life which this blessing implies, and yet we cannot deny that our desire to see, to know, and to touch seems to stand in the way of receiving the fullness of this blessing.

But the mystery is this: that we already see; on the other hand, there is much in us which wants to touch and see the wounds of Christ. This is a perfectly legitimate desire because after all we are going to be at Christ's banquet forever, where he gives himself to us as life itself. Why shouldn't we want to touch him?

Why is faith so hard then? Because we are so shortsighted. The life of Christ is so real, so deep, so full of radiance, that even while we are in it it escapes us. The mystery of the Christian life is that stumbling fidelity of growing into Christ in whom somehow we already are.

If we knew how humble and how gentle the Lord Jesus was, and how much he loved us, we would be able to have the effrontery of Thomas. After making his out-landish statement, he at least showed up on the Octave with the other apostles. If we realize that we exist by the mercy of God, then we begin to grasp that the mystery of faith and life is already at work in us. We often don't see this—not because it isn't present—but because the presence of so many other things obscures our knowledge of it.

In our life the Spirit of God is moving us. The Christian life is not acquiring something, getting hold of something. It is realizing that at this moment we are already in possession of a great treasure. If sometimes we feel like Thomas, maybe that very feeling is our witness. The world is full of Thomases. If we find him in ourselves or in others we should say, "Do you really want to see Christ, touch him? You will, but with the sight, touch, and embrace that is deeper and more beautiful than any human touching can imagine."

"And these words are written that we can believe that Jesus is the Son of God and through this faith have life in his name." This is John's last word to us. We need not be afraid of being Thomases, if only we persevere in our desire to see and to touch Christ, and admit how imperfect is our understanding of what touch and sight really are.

If we really desire to see Jesus, then we will have the courage to loosen our grasp on every sight and touch which does not give us contact with the Risen Lord. We will loosen our grasp on all those things which only give us a temporary and frustrating sense of security. Then our desire will be real, and when Christ appears we will realize how deeply the mystery of his life is at work in us. When he comes we will recognize him and be able to say, "My Lord and my God."

At that meeting we will know the meaning of blessedness. It is true even in this life that though we are God's children, it has not yet appeared to us what we shall be. For we shall see him as we allow the desire to see him transform us, so that we are like him. Then we shall know the love of Christ which surpasses understanding, and even amid the darkness and weakness of this life, we shall know the radiant joy of this last beatitude, "Blessed are those who have not seen but have believed."